yellow P
3300

DRAGON MOM
CONFESSIONS OF A CHILD DEVELOPMENT EXPERT

by
Janet Gonzalez-Mena

Illustrated by Leon Cor

Rattle OK Publications
Napa, California

DRAGON MOM:
Confessions of a Child Development Expert
by
Janet Gonzalez-Mena

Published by :
Rattle OK Publications
P.O. Box 5614
Napa CA 94581-0614

All rights reserved. No part of this book may be reproduced or transmitted in any form or by any means, electronic or mechanical, including information storage and retrieval systems without written permission from the publisher, except for quotations selected by reviewers.

Printed and bound in the United States of America.
10 9 8 7 6 5 4 3 2 1

Library of Congress Cataloging-in-Publication Data
Gonzalez-Mena, Janet, 1937–
Dragon Mom/by Janet Gonzalez-Mena

                                                95-67948
                                                CIP

Copyright © 1995 by Rattle OK Publications
ISBN 1-883965-29-2

Illustrated by Leon Contorno

"Thanks to Janet Gonzalez-Mena, the secret is out: parenting is a powerfully passionate business and it should be. DRAGON MOM is for every parent who suspects that somewhere inside lurks a fire-breathing dragon that shouldn't be there."
    Amy Dombro, author
    THE ORDINARY IS EXTRAORDINARY

"I laughed and cried and was deeply touched by this personal parenting story,...a wonderful lesson about the healing power of getting in touch with passion, no matter how awful it may look."
    Carolyn Miller, facilitator of Living in Process Groups for
        Anne Wilson Schaef
    Director, Work Systems by Design

"Janet's gift for telling stories on herself, and her expertise in analyzing them, yields both a model of the quest for self-understanding and a wealth of splendid advice (which she cheerfully admits she doesn't follow). As another child development expert and mother of many, I recognized myself. Lovely book!"
    Elizabeth Jones, author
    EMERGENT CURRICULUM

"A thoughtful and honest look at the passion behind parenting and the challenge of merging theory and practice...Should be mandatory reading for child care providers..
    Louis Torelli
    Early childhood and design specialist

"Fantastic! Made me laugh and made me think...a realistic view of being a parent...It's a book that should be read by both parents and people who work with parents."
    Anne Willis Stonehouse, author and editor
    TRUSTING TODDLERS
    GOOD BEGINNINGS FOR BABIES

Dedicated to my children
Bruce, Bret, Robin, Adam, and Tim

May they forgive me for my parenting blunders
and for any misperceptions in my storytelling

ACKNOWLEDGEMENTS

This book is based on my own experience, and a loose interpretation of many theories, especially Psychosynthesis and Transactional Analysis. I want to acknowledge Pam Levin (*Becoming the Way We Are: A Transactional Guide to Personal Development*) and Jean Isley Clark (*Self-Esteem: A Family Affair*). I was influenced by Roberto Assaginoli's *Psychosynthesis: A Manual of Principles and Techniques* and send thanks to Jane Vennard for helping me long ago with Psychosynthesis concepts.

I learned about Rudolf Dreikurs' use of consequences when I read *Children the Challenge* and was touched by Thomas Gordon's approach to communication in his book *Parent Effectiveness Training.*

Magda Gerber, who isn't as interested in theories and theorists as in authenticity, helped me see the importance of accepting myself as I am. I want to acknowledge Stephen Nelson for continuing to encourage me to get *Dragon Mom* published. I am grateful to Heather Wallach and Lynne Lyle, whose parenting experiences have sparked many memories in me which were helpful in the writing of this book. Most of all, I wish to thank Sharon Elwell and her Rattle OK Publications for taking Dragon Mom, the manuscript, and turning it into *Dragon Mom*, the book.

TABLE OF CONTENTS

INTRODUCTION

INTRODUCTION

I like being seen as a child development expert. When I step to the podium or autograph my books, I feel calm and competent. How I wish my children could meet that person!

✳✳✳✳✳✳✳✳✳✳

It was a warm October afternoon. Halloween was just a few days away. I was holed up in the back room with my computer, working on an article for *TWINS* magazine about how to get kids to pick up messes. My youngest son, then seven, and his friend were busy with a box of leftover Halloween costumes they had found in the attic.

The writing was coming easily. I have many ideas about getting children to do what you want them to do. It would have been simple to finish a first draft if there hadn't been so many interruptions.

"Mom, can you fasten this for me?"

"Mom, Ricky wants to know if he can wear Dad's hat."

"Mom, can you get that Halloween puzzle down from the top of the closet for us?"

"Mom, where are my crayons?"

"Mom, we can't think of anything to do!"

Finally, desperate for some quiet, I suggested the boys carve pumpkins, knowing it would take a long time. I set them up in the kitchen, spreading newspaper on the table. I supplied pumpkins, scooping utensils, and safe little saws for cutting. Then I returned to the computer.

They were quiet for a very long time. Even a beginning parent knows that silence is a bad sign, a warning signal. But I chose to be thankful instead of warned. I finished the first draft of my article and started in on a second draft without interruption. When I emerged much later, I was greeted with a gross, sticky floor, pumpkin seeds everywhere, and the table and counter loaded with a variety of disgusting utensils covered with orange slime.

I wasn't surprised. I knew I had bought my writing time and I expected to pay a price. However, I had just written that it is important for parents to "stay on top of messes" and to "make sure children take responsibility for their own cleanup." The contrast between what I had written and what I had done was too great to ignore. My article made no mention of buying time.

Leaving the kitchen as it was, I went looking for the boys–not to get them to clean up, but to be sure they were all right. Hearing their voices in the living room, I peeked in, knowing that I would see a big mess. Sure enough. Across the rug lay about two hundred blocks sprinkled with action figures. This "base" was the result of several days' work. I had purposely refrained from making my son pick up the blocks after the first day of construction. I knew from experience that building, rebuilding, and modifying a structure was much more satisfying than starting from scratch each time.

My article, however, stated that it was important for children to pick up after themselves right away. I had violated my own principle–not accidentally, but intentionally. Since the boys were playing contentedly, I went back into isolation and rewrote the article, this time being less simplistic and more truthful.

I was feeling good about how my expert self could learn from my parent self. As I watched the last page of copy come from my printer, I felt entirely satisfied. I turned off the computer. I was ready to deal with the mess.

Walking out of the room, I suddenly realized that the house was quiet again. This time, I took the warning. I sensed something was amiss. My heart started thumping. Where were the boys? I rushed into the living room. The blocks were still there, but no boys. I followed a trial of cracker crumbs leading into the hall where a squashed box lay, spilling more crackers and crumbs onto the rug. Beyond, I saw a race track ascending the stairs. A sprinkling of small cars lay at the bottom of the stairs among the broken crackers.

I continued following the trail of destruction up the steps, avoiding broken crayons, ripped papers, and banana peels. I reminded myself that I had been buying precious writing time, but my breath was coming in short gasps and I could feel my face getting red.

My heart was leaping as I stood before the closed attic door. I could hear smothered giggles. I slowly reached for the doorknob, hesitating before turning it. Then I opened the door wide and peered into the gloom.

Remembering the scene behind that door can still bring tears to my eyes. Standing on bent and scattered books, the precious contents of a tipped-over bookcase, the two boys were busy emptying cardboard boxes of outgrown clothes and baby toys onto each other. And they were laughing about it!

I stood silently in the doorway. They stopped, turning to look at me. I took a deep breath, then another. Each inhalation inflated my body. The boys' eyes widened as they watched me transform. My head shrank as my body puffed up to three times normal size. Behind me grew a huge, crusty tail. Giant wings sprouted from my shoulders. My eyes became small and beady. My mouth expanded around to my eyes and filled up with sharp pointed teeth.

When the transformation was complete, I stood on my hind legs, waving my front legs with their deadly claws in the faces of the terrified boys. Fire issued from my mouth in a roar that filled the small attic to bursting.

"What are you two doing?" The question was superfluous. All three of us knew what they were doing. A dramatic pause allowed me to

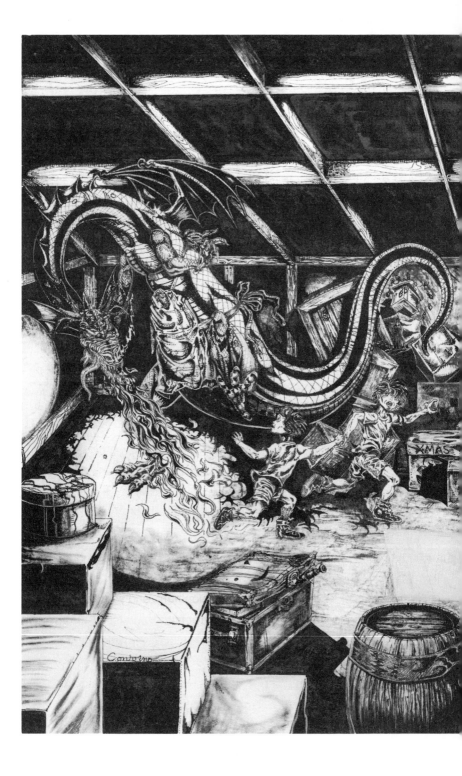

gather more breath so that I was still roaring as I continued. "That's the last straw! I've been nice to you all afternoon. And what do I get for it!?"

I started toward them, crushing everything in my path. I lifted a gigantic hind foot, threatening to place it squarely on my son's head. Grabbing Ricky's hand, he ducked out between my legs and the two of them disappeared down the stairs.

※※※※※※※※※※

My son and I know from experience that my threats are worse than my actions. I may seem to be out of control, but I have a safety switch that turns on when this dragon reaches her peak—just before she actually strikes. She threatens to inflict damage, but she never follows through.

Safe though this creature may be, she's a source of continual embarrassment to me. I try not to let anyone know of her existence, but here I am telling about her. I'd prefer to appear as a calm, competent expert at child-rearing. Unfortunately, my secret is out. Sometimes I don't look or sound anything like the person writing these words. I'm glad no one else was in the attic that day to see me!

The next part is just as embarrassing to confess: I spent the rest of the afternoon cleaning up that mess by myself. And this is the same person who spent the first part of the afternoon writing an article on how to get children to pick up their own messes!

When I first decided to write this book, I never dreamed it would be about Dragon Mom. I intended to write a parenting book full of advice from my store of knowledge and my many years of experience. After five children, a master's degree in human development, and years of teaching experience, I know a lot about parenting.

But when I actually sat down to begin the preaching, the attic monster took control of my hands. Suddenly, I found that I was telling on myself.

The truth is, I've almost never been the loving, calm, rational parent I want to be. More often, I am a dragon. But dragons are not always mean—just big, powerful, and clumsy. We don't get mean unless we're hurt or threatened.

Many parents have an irrational dragon in them, and many parents wish they didn't. They also have a voice of reason. The trick is to get one to talk to the other—to build a bridge between the two. You can only do that if you acknowledge the dragon. It has taken me a long time to see that.

I spent years trying to kill off my dragon, or at least make her disappear. It seemed possible to me to parent from reason alone. I know now that it would never work. I need feelings to parent—not just happy ones, but all sorts of feelings. Parenting is (and should be) powerfully passionate business.

Denying the dragon allows her to rage on unchecked until she reaches the point of triggering the safety switch. That safety switch is my voice of reason. Not all parents have one, and for them it is even more vital to get in touch with the dragon within them. Without the safety switch, it becomes imperative that the dragon be prevented from doing real damage. And it's impossible to tame or control a monster if you refuse to believe it exists!

When Dragon Mom goes into a rage, I have trouble hearing the voice of reason because of all the static on the line in the form of self-criticism.

"You shouldn't yell at your kids that way!"

"You should be kind and understanding."

"You should be firm and consistent."

"You shouldn't get so upset."

"You should be reasonable."

Well, I'm not reasonable very often, and I've finally come to see that's okay. Parenting is not a reasonable occupation. People parent from the gut, not the head, and that's as it should be. Passion and spontaneity are essential to parenting. You need real feelings to be a parent.

In me, those passionate feelings come mainly from the dragon. A lot of her passion is anger, but the intensity of her anger is a demonstration of her capacity for love. If she gets the love and respect she needs from me, she'll be able to give more love to her children. I firmly believe it, but it's hard to love a monster you've always hated!

When I say feelings are important, I'm not advising that you disregard your head altogether. You can learn useful things with your head and put them into effect in parenting. You can cultivate the voice of reason, make friends with it, until it becomes an asset to you. You need your head. But not to the exclusion of feelings.

The public expects a lot from parenting experts. Since we know so much, we should do a better job of parenting, right? Wrong. Knowing about something doesn't insure that you will act on that knowledge. I'm a good example. I'd probably be better off to know less and use it more.

A theme of this book is the contrast between what I know and what I do. I'm telling you this because I think you'll recognize yourself as a parent and maybe we'll both quit kicking ourselves.

I've learned a lot in thirty years of parenting. But I'm still working on the most important lesson–to love and forgive myself.

So here you have the true confessions of an early childhood educator. This book is about the dark side of parenting, but it's also about the lighter side. I hope you'll learn something you can use. I hope you'll feel better about yourself as a parent. I do–now that I've finally confessed!

> *What I know:* I am made up of a number of parenting parts. There is no one real me who parents. Though this is Dragon Mom's book, she isn't the only parent me.
>
> *What I do:* I forget that there is no one real me! I dislike, even hate, some of my parenting parts–especially Dragon Mom. Instead of accepting them, I want to replace them with the image of the perfect parent that I carry around in my head. I don't give my less-than-perfect parts a chance to grow and be the best that they can be. I forget that each of them is built around positive energy and that it is only through distortion that they act in hurtful ways.
>
> *Why:* I am still in the process of growing and developing. I will never be finished. I am less than perfect. I'm a human being.

CHAPTER ONE
ABOUT BEING REAL

This book is about being who you really are. Many parenting books take into account your not-nice aspects, but subtly give the message that you should be nice–or if not nice, at least reasonable and calm. My experience is that the effect of that message is guilt. This book is different. I urge you to be yourself when you parent, and to like it! I know that's easier said than done.

The parent me has several aspects. I've already shown you Dragon Mom in the introduction. As you get to know her, you'll see that she plays a variety of roles. She blows up. She also protects those around her, structuring situations to keep her young offspring from harm. She's not always obvious about this task of hers.

Even when she's not blowing up, she's oversized, which results in clumsiness. Her brain is minute, which results in more automatic behavior and less thoughtful behavior. It's hard to believe, but basically she is a lovable character, innocent and good at heart in spite of her nasty temper and her potential for destruction.

> *Dragon Mom is good at heart in spite of her nasty temper.*

I have another parenting character. I call her Mrs. Bodunky. She's almost the opposite of Dragon Mom. A sweet, kindly, plump, nurturing person, she likes to make delicious meals and gets great satisfaction out of watching people eat them. When she cuddles her offspring, she's warm, soft, and smells of lavender soap. She sings lullabies and cheery wake-up songs instead of screaming, "Go to bed!" or "Get up!" as Dragon Mom has been known to do.

Like Dragon Mom, Mrs. Bodunky has her bad side. The dragon's potential for destruction is evident. Her size alone means that she could crush a child with a single footstep. Her claws are capable of bloody gashes which heal into scars. She has a strict hands-off rule when she's angry, but all of us are aware of the lethal potential. Mrs. Bodunky's potential for destruction is less obvious.

> *Like Dragon Mom, Mrs. Bodunky has her bad side.*

Mrs. Bodunky puffs up as the dragon does, but instead of turning into a monster, she turns into a marshmallowy ooze. Though she still looks like a kindly plump woman, when she embraces a child, there is danger of suffocation. I don't know if you have ever been embraced by marshmallow ooze, but it can be pretty awful. Some kids like it because it's soft and sweet. The suffocation effect is so subtle that sometimes children don't even know it's happening.

Here is an example of puffed-up Bodunky:

2

3 Contorno 94

****

"Mommy, I hurt my knee." Child, who has been waiting all day for attention from busy mother working on a magazine article, presents a dirty knee with an infinitesimal red mark.

"Oh, poor baby!" Scoops up child in arms, carrying off to bathroom. Washes knee while gushing sympathy. Gives child several band-aids. Takes back to kitchen. Feeds. Gives present she was saving for upcoming birthday. Leaves child to play with present and returns to computer.

Like Dragon Mom, Bodunky's brain is on the small side and she operates on automatic pilot a good deal of the time. But at her core she is as good and innocent as her monster counterpart.

****

Here is the dragon in the same situation: "What do you mean you're hurt? That's just a tiny scratch. Did you clean up your room yet?"

"But the hurt is inside. I think my leg is broken!"

"Don't be silly. Your leg isn't broken. You're standing on it. It's in fine shape to take out the trash, which I see is overflowing."

Child picks up leg, trying to balance on one foot. "I need a band-aid."

"Don't be ridiculous. That little scratch doesn't need anything. What you need is to do what I told you and quit bugging me about little things." Voice raises.

"This isn't a little thing."

"Of course it is. Quit fussing and do your chores." Voice is now screaming.

****

I'll spare you the rest of the scene. Eventually the child either gives up or Dragon Mom starts feeling guilty about her anger. That guilty feeling may lead to an apology to the child. After the apology, she turns

4

the child in question over to Bodunky to smother with marshmallow cream.

As you see, the two often work in concert. The dragon appears—arguing, screaming, threatening, and criticizing. When she is finished, she invites Mrs. Bodunky to take over. That dear woman then mops up by doing for the children whatever Dragon Mom had wanted them to do. The attic scene in the introduction is an example of this situation.

Both of these characters have good qualities. They just don't behave very well. Dragon Mom combines strength, power, and determination. Bodunky, in her warm, accepting way, can be appropriately nurturing if she doesn't blow up into a marshmallow.

I want you to know that in addition to these two characters I have a mature, intelligent, thoughtful, competent parent in me. She has a normal-sized brain and doesn't operate on automatic pilot. She listens to the voice of reason regularly, although she still has feelings and expresses them.

I like to think of this person as the real me, but of course she's not. She's just one of us. I like so much to think of her as me that I call her Janet, although her real name is Janet Competent Parent, or Janet C. Parent. Unfortunately, J.C.P. isn't around most of the time when I'm parenting. These other two bunglers keep appearing.

I do want to show how Janet C. Parent would have handled the bumped knee situation, so I'm giving her a little space.

❋❋❋❋❋❋❋❋❋❋

"Mommy, I hurt my knee."

Mommy looks up from the computer and says, "Well, I see you have a little red mark there." Puts arm around child and gets down at eye level so they are talking face to face.

"I hurt myself."

5

"I know you've been playing by yourself for a long time now, while I've been working on the computer."

"Yeah, and then I fell down."

"I bet you'd like me to spend some time with you for a while. Why don't you wash off your knee and then we'll decide what to do together." Waits to see if child moves toward bathroom. Child remains still. "Do you want me to help you wash your knee?"

※※※※※※※※※※

The above behavior is what I've learned how to do. I can be calm and realistic. I can be understanding and appropriately nurturing. I can be adult and mature without being empty or unreal. I don't do those things naturally. I've learned to do them. I've learned from books, from classes, and from watching other competent parents.

I find it easy to like myself when I'm Janet Competent Parent. But I know that I'm more likely to be the dragon or Bodunky in a given situation. These people in me all have personalities. Each has a certain consistency, which means that she thinks, feels, and acts in fairly predictable ways. Each speaks in a different voice.

> *Each of the people in me has a distinct voice and personality.*

All of these characters are part of the real me. When I am one of them I may not be nice, but I am being real. I can also make up characters and be a fake. I'm at my fakest when someone who expects me to be an expert is present when I'm with my children. I am aware that this happens, but awareness doesn't seem to help. I wasn't always aware of my own fakeness. One of my children taught me about it.

※※※※※※※※※※

I was finishing up my first day as a preschool teacher when my three-year-old son arrived from the class next door. He kept tugging on my apron as he waited for me to say good-bye to my remaining students. I could see that he was impatient to ask me something. Finally, I turned and asked, "What is it, Adam?"

"Mommy....?" He looked puzzled.

"Yes?" His next words stunned me. I've never forgotten them.

"Why were you talking so funny to those kids?"

✸✸✸✸✸✸✸✸✸✸

I realized at that moment that I had been trying hard to be true to my concept of a real teacher. I was being more of a smiley face than a real person. I can certainly forgive myself for that phony behavior. I was new at this job. I didn't know how to be "me" and "teacher" both. I was playing a superficial role – and not very well, either.

I got better as I got more experience. I developed a "teacher" set of characteristics that were closer to who I really am than the smiley-faced exterior I used as a beginner.

My teacher me is different from my parent me. But she has the full range of characteristics: I can be as nurturing, protecting, critical, marshmallowy, or as calm, mature, and reasonable a teacher as I am a parent. Nevertheless, I feel and act differently when the children I am in charge of are not my own.

Unfortunately, I seldom get such clear and immediate feedback when I'm being fake as I got from Adam that day long ago. I have had to work on distinguishing "realness" for myself. I've found that my "fake detector" works better detecting fakeness in others than it does picking out my own.

> *My fake detector works better on others than on myself!*

But periodically, I can call forth that three-year-old voice asking his very serious question. I'm also getting better at listening to my voice of

7

reason when it says, "You're being fake, Janet." The trick is to take a split second from what might be an emotional moment and really listen.

Children need to be raised by real people, not fakes playing superficial roles. They need full-bodied people, not inflatable life-sized dolls like "Mama Smiley Face," who is nothing but a shell.

My Bodunky with her marshmallow insides is better than a parent with nothing inside. Fakes are empty shells. Poke them hard enough and they collapse. Shells are empty because their real feelings are hidden away. Children need parents who show the many aspects of themselves.

Parents who are home all day every day with their children have little chance to play superficial roles, to be fakes, to operate as shells. The time factor works against that. Constant togetherness forces people to be real. But most of today's parents have limited time with their children, and so may strive harder to maintain a smiley-faced parent shell, because they think they should. The pressure of making time together into "quality time" leads to fake roles.

Usually parents can't achieve the smiley-faced shell for very long. They feel guilty when the shell collapses and real feelings appear – feelings that aren't always "nice." They don't appreciate the fact that it's better for their kids to see them acting mean, tired, grouchy, and impatient than it is for them to feel that way and act some other way.

A test of realness is asking, "What's happening inside me right now?" When you ask that question, you get in touch with your physical and emotional feelings, and become aware that you have some choices. One choice is to be honest about your reactions.

The voice asking the question, "What's happening inside me?" and making the choice is called "the self". The voice of reason is part of that self. But the self isn't just a voice or a person; it's more of a control center. If you dislike the dehumanized electronic image, you can personify it by thinking of it as the director of all your parts.

The director is nothing alone. It must always be clothed in personality. It cannot act without a role. Just as you can't act without a body, neither can you act without a personality – a set of roles. The word "personality" comes from the word "persona," which means "mask." That's not to say that we all walk around hidden behind masks; the message is just the opposite. The mask doesn't hide you; it allows you to be in the world, to act, to express yourself, to feel. It gives shape to the shapeless, animates, gives voice. Without a mask, there is no real you. The self behind these masks or roles doesn't act; it only directs. It chooses which aspect of your personality will come forth at any given moment.

Being real doesn't mean acting straight out of the self. It means being aware of the self at the center, and the self being aware of the full range of "you's." This has to do with knowing that there is a controlling factor beyond the actor of the moment. This control center has the well-being of the individual at heart and aims at meeting that individual's needs. The director, or self, operates the safety switch that keeps the dragon from abusing her children.

Each of us has the lifelong task of expressing all these parts of ourselves. Most of us don't like all our parts, which is understandable, because not all of them are nice. I truly hate the dragon most of the time. Some parts of all of us have inevitably been warped and twisted as we were growing up. One of the tasks of the adult is to come to know and accept all these parts.

I'm working hard with Dragon Mom. Writing this book is one of the ways I'm getting in touch with her. I'm hoping that all the attention will help her express her good qualities more and her warped, destructive qualities less. I firmly believe that all my parts are basically good. Each holds valuable energy. I can't use this energy as long as I deny, neglect, or try to kill off the parts of me that I don't like.

As parents, we need to be fully who we are so that our children can learn how to feel feelings, express them, make choices, and recognize needs. They will more easily learn to be real if their parents are real. They will learn to deny parts of themselves if they see that behavior in their parents' example. They will play superficial, stereotypical roles if the people around them play those kinds of roles. Being real is accepting and sometimes expressing all the parts of you. Being real is being fully yourself even if you don't always like yourself. Being real is being grouchy and impatient sometimes, warm and accepting sometimes, angry and intense sometimes, needy sometimes, giving sometimes. Children need parents who are all of these – and more.

> *Children need real people to raise them - not fakes!*

What I know:	My anger contains energy I can use to express myself and to make things happen. I can direct the energy to work on the problem that is the source of the anger. I can work towards solutions that don't tear down or intentionally hurt others. My anger can give me extra strength and insight so that a problem I can't handle becomes solvable with the angry energy.
What I do:	I blow up, stew, stuff it, yell, cry, hurt. None of these expressions of anger are very effective at getting my needs met or making changes.
Why:	I'm acting out old patterns. My needs are twisted. I'm human—and I'm a dragon.

CHAPTER TWO
ANGER

Since this is Dragon Mom's book, it is filled with anger. Each chapter has anger imbedded in it. Few people warn you that anger is part of parenting, bound to rear its ugly head on a regular basis. Anger plays a part in almost everyone's life, but somehow parental anger is bigger and uglier than other kinds.

My anger, you know by now, often comes out in the dragon. It sometimes seems as if she's made up of anger – that she's composed of nothing but wild, overblown emotion. Janet Competent Parent also feels anger at times, but hers stays in proportion and is appropriately expressed.

How well I remember Dragon Mom's first angry appearance! Just like in a movie, a single event triggered her awakening.

11

> *The dragon mom was suddenly awakened.*

I was new to my parenting career. The dragon was unknown to me. So far, parenting had been entirely positive. I felt nothing but love in my heart for this precious new child of mine. I certainly didn't feel anger. I remember thinking this was the happiest time in my life.

You can imagine how surprised I felt to find myself in the living room of our small apartment screaming, "Shut up!" in the direction of the bedroom where my baby lay crying. I swear those words just came out of my mouth on their own.

I had been a "good mother" up until then–all three weeks of his life. My baby had responded by behaving like a "good baby." But not this time. I had done everything right. I had changed, fed, burped, rocked, and cuddled him. He just wouldn't stop crying.

That moment of frustration brought ugly, unmotherly words out of my mouth. When I heard them, I was nearly crushed by the overpowering weight of tons of guilt crashing down on me. Only a strong, monster's body could withstand that weight!

I don't remember what happened next, but I'm willing to bet that I called forth Mrs. Bodunky, who went right in and smothered that poor baby in marshmallow ooze. I don't know if my sugary glop stopped the crying or not, but I probably felt better. That was the real beginning of my parenting career.

Throughout the childhood years of my children, anger has been a constant, ugly presence. No one can make me as angry as my offspring–those beings I love beyond description. I chose this way of life. I didn't fall into motherhood accidentally. I can't even imagine how much more angry I might have been if I hadn't wanted to be a mother! Why was I mad so often? Why was I a dragon instead of my sweet image of what a

12

mother should be?

It has taken me years to understand where Dragon Mom came from. I know now that she started more than a half century ago as something I call "the wild animal," who is an angry child inside of me. The history of my anger is my own history, but perhaps if I tell you the story of my anger, you'll be stirred to look at the roots of your own. All adult anger has its roots in childhood, and a history.

> *Adult anger comes from childhood history.*

I have always known about my "wild animal." Events in her history that I don't actually remember have been recounted to me many times. They say that I was a "good girl," even as a tiny baby – remarkably "good." However, I had one little flaw. It didn't happen often, but occasionally the "good girl" would have a rather spectacular tantrum. I must have made quite an impression, because I've heard about these outbursts since I can remember.

At some point, I made an unconscious decision to cage up this wild animal of my babyhood, and I did an excellent job. She did manage to break out of her pen periodically during my childhood. I remember some of her crying, screaming rages. It was carefully pointed out to me that they were always over "nothing."

My angry child self was locked up tighter and tighter until she barely appeared at all. The tantrums virtually stopped when I reached adulthood. However, once I became a parent, Dragon Mom appeared and my angry child once more began to express herself openly. And loudly. And dramatically.

All my children know Dragon Mom very well. But I continue to keep her caged around adults. One day I discovered just how I do this.

13

I was forty years old, no youngster, sitting in the meeting of my graduate committee. I had submitted my nearly-complete master's project earlier, and we were gathered to discuss it. I had foolishly expected nothing but praise, so I was astounded to hear critical voices coming at me. The project, a guide for infant caregivers, was something on which I had worked long and hard. I was very proud of it, and confident that it would meet with approval.

"This sounds patronizing to me," said one committee member.

"And this part isn't clear," added another.

"You have some contradictions here..." pointed out the first.

"And here..." said the second.

I listened stunned. For a split second, the dragon woke up. She threatened to stomp and roar. But as fast as that creature is, the director is faster. The dragon was caged so quickly that no one in the room—including me—was aware of her brief presence. I didn't realize this sequence had even happened until later.

My director immediately replaced the big monster with a poor helpless little girl who dissolved into tears, melting the hearts of these powerful people who had so recently been critical. Even now, years later, I can feel my face flush with embarrassment as I write about this. I was hugged and comforted, feeling like a fool in the midst of my tears.

✳✳✳✳✳✳✳✳✳✳

Later, as I learned more about the various components of my personality, I was able to see that situation more clearly. There had been three me's present in that room, and they had appeared in a predictable pattern that is very familiar to me. The first was an adult, the one who later became the expert. Even then she was a competent writer and she entered the room with confidence.

The second, who appeared and left so quickly that I was not even aware of her, was the dragon, who felt attacked and responded like an angry child.

The third was Pitiful Precious, a poor little girl who managed to deflect criticism and receive nurturing from these powerful people whom the dragon had not been allowed to confront. Indeed, my director was right. Releasing the dragon might have wreaked havoc. She's trustworthy with her own children, but she's had so little practice with adults that she might have left others wounded. There's no telling what she might have done!

It has been suggested to me that the angry child, my wild animal, is too risky in her pure form, and that the pitiful girl is the manipulative aspect of the same creature: the two aren't really separate. Intellectually I can buy that concept, but emotionally I still feel their separateness. I can imagine that one day the two will become integrated and the energy that each holds will be available for meeting my needs and serving the good. In the meantime, I'm still dealing with this old, old pattern when I feel both angry and powerless around adults.

The pattern changes around my children. Dragon Mom seldom turns into poor little Pitiful Precious. Playing for sympathy never worked with my children. If you are a parent, you know that most children just don't feel sorry, no matter how pitiful their parents act.

> *Pitiful Precious is ineffective with children.*

"Darling, please quit making so much noise. Mommy has a terrible headache!"

"Mommy --headache?.." Yell, yell, bang, bang, scream, scream.

There's no point in parading a pitiful child in front of my children. Instead, here is how the pattern has developed. Dragon Mom blows up, puts on a magnificent performance, feels guilty, and then turns into inflated Mrs. Bodunky, who proceeds to overindulge the child who was the focus of the dragon's wrath.

We're all used to Dragon Mom in our family, and no one fears her. Even when she's angry and appears to be out of control, we're all confident that she knows when to stop. She makes a lot of noise, but when the dust dies down, everyone is still intact. She can wound – especially when she blames and criticizes – but she's so big and out of proportion to reality that she is seldom taken seriously. She embarrasses me, I have to admit. I'd rather not look or sound like a monster. But I don't fear her because I know her so well. I can trust her.

> *Stewing is a dangerous way to handle anger.*

Besides the dragon blow-ups, I have another way to handle my angry energy – one I'm so ashamed of that I wish I didn't have to mention it. I stew. I'm a great stewer. I can take just a few simple ingredients and create a glorious bubbling cauldron of potentially lethal mess deep inside myself. I add spices by talking to other people – not the one at whom the anger is directed. I look very adult while I'm stewing, except that I become quiet and less communicative. This is an ugly pattern. In comparison to this one, Dragon-Bodunky or Dragon-Poor Precious patterns look positively wonderful!

Intellectually, I am aware that anger holds a lot of energy that I can use in positive ways. I can confront and problem-solve, and find ways to express anger that won't harm others or leave me vulnerable. Janet Competent Parent is good at expressing anger so that it gets a positive effect.

> *Anger can be used to make positive changes.*

"You said this morning that if I drove you to school you were going to put your things away as soon as you got home this afternoon. But now I see you sprawled out in front of the TV and the mess is still on the floor."

"Yeah, Mom. I'm going to do it as soon as this program is over."

"No. We had an agreement. You said right after school. That's now!"

"Yeah, yeah. I'll do it. Quit bugging me!"

"I don't like it when you talk to me like that."

"Well, then lay off me!"

"No. We had an agreement."

"Well, I'm not going to do it now, and you can't make me!"

"I feel really angry when you say that to me! I don't expect to have to make you. I expect you to carry out your part of the agreement."

Mom is standing in front of TV. Child is forced to look at her instead of the picture. Child figures if he pushes a little further he can trigger the dragon-Bodunky reaction.

"Geeze, Mom, lay off!" He tries to look around her at the TV. She snaps it off, comes near to him, looks him right in the eye. Her look says, "I mean business, and I'm not going to give up or blow up."

"I don't see what difference a few minutes is going to make." Child slouches off the couch and reluctantly picks up one dirty sock.

"It makes a difference to me."

✳✳✳✳✳✳✳✳✳✳

I'm really proud of myself when I persist and don't fall back on the old patterns of making a fuss and then feeling guilty and overcompensating. Janet Competent Parent can use angry energy to persist until something happens. I can do that with my children, and also with the rest of the world. If I could remember that fact at emotional

17

moments, I could reduce my more familiar patterns of stewing or getting hurt, pouting, and hoping to get hugged.

> *We can choose how to use anger.*

One important thing to remember about anger is that you don't have to <u>do</u> anything about it. You don't have to express it by letting it out. You don't have to repress it by stuffing it in, either. You can choose to simply feel it–really feel it. If you can learn to do this for varying lengths of time, you can make better decisions about whether you want to act on your anger.

Staying with a feeling is not easy for me. I am a master at unconsciously distracting myself, or exchanging one feeling for another, like moving from anger to self-pity or from anger to guilt. Sometimes that ability to change feelings is useful–like when I'm afraid and I need to act bravely. But mostly it narrows my life and makes me a less complete person. Someone said that feelings are like the chords on an organ. You can choose to play only a few, but you limit your music.

Since I learned all this, some changes have occured in me. I call upon my angry dragon less as I have begun to acknowledge my feelings. I have been aware for years that I blew up at my offspring more frequently when outside pressures were greater. I have carried a great deal of guilt about this one! Now, I am better able to put anger that belongs in the outside world in its proper place. Coincidentally, only one of my children is still living at home. Maybe that's a factor. Perhaps now that fewer little people are around, I'm forced to deal with the true sources of anger.

Interestingly, people began to use words like "mellow," "low-key," "calm,"–even "serene!"–to describe me once I began to acknowledge and accept my dragon. I no longer have to use energy to hide her.

Here's a last word about anger. Sometimes anger is less a result of what is happening than a desire for an intense interaction. We all remember those wonderful intimate moments in our lives when we really connected with someone. In most lives those times are few and far between. But an argument gives a sense of connectedness, of intensity, of passion. When I'm fighting I don't feel the warm glow of the wonderful moments, but I do feel involved in something that really matters. I may not feel love in the connection, but I do feel intensity in the interaction. I feel the strength of the emotion. It's one time I can count on the full attention of the person I'm engaged with. Keep this in mind reading the next chapter about arguments.

Whatever else my anger is, it's real! Whenever I deny it, I'm bound to act like a fake. Realness comes from accepting anger and then deciding whether to express it, act on it, or just acknowledge that it's there.

What I know:	I know how to fight fair and how to clear the air of my anger. I know how to distinguish arguments which are mine from those which belong to other people. I know how to respond to the arguments of others by helping them express their feelings, problem-solve, and clear the air of their anger. I know that anger and arguing are ways to get attention. I know that anger and arguing are ways to achieve an intense interaction.
What I do:	I fight dirty or refuse to fight when it's my argument. When it's not my argument, I often ignore what's going on. I may run away, get mad, or use pushy power to make things happen.
Why :	I'm a dragon. I don't think about what is going on, but just react whenever one of my buttons is pushed. If I get involved in my children's arguments inappropriately, I may feel a need to get mad and fight. If I run away, I am lacking in energy or interest, or feeling powerless.

CHAPTER THREE
ARGUMENTS

I am trying to solve an argument between my 4- and 6-year-olds:

✳✳✳✳✳✳✳✳✳✳

"Give that back! It's mine!"

"Get your hands off it or I'll tell Mom!"

"Go ahead! It's mine!" Gives brother a shove.

"I had it first!" Screams.

"MOM!"

Mom arrives on the scene. "Okay, children, that's enough

arguing. Give it back to your brother."

"But I had it first!" Clutches toy desperately.

"You can play with this one." Offers alternative toy.

"But…"

"Nyaa, nyaa. Told you so!"

Dragon Mom appears. "Stop it right now, both of you! That's it! I can't stand all this bickering. Don't either one of you dare open your mouth again, or I'll do something so horrible that you can't even imagine what it is!"

✳✳✳✳✳✳✳✳✳✳

It would never end there, of course. They'd keep on and I'd keep trying to assert my power. I was never very effective at stopping arguments by trying to show the arguing parties that I was more powerful than they were. We all knew that wasn't true. They were the powerful ones. They always sucked me in and I often ended up blithering and fussing more than they.

> *Instead of assuming a power stance, a parent can be a problem-solving facilitator.*

When I began teaching preschool, I learned another way to handle my children's arguments. Instead of taking a power stance, I arrived as a problem-solving facilitator. Instead of involving myself, I could remain emotionally detached. I learned how to get arguing parties to talk to each other instead of appealing to me. I learned how to help them express feelings. I learned how to keep them engaged with each other until a solution was reached or the situation was defused.

Magda Gerber, a Los Angeles infant specialist who was a teacher of mine, calls this process "sports announcing" instead of refereeing. Here's a sample of a preschool teacher handling the same situation as a "sports announcer:"

✳✳✳✳✳✳✳✳✳✳

"Give that back! It's mine!"

"Get your hands off it or I'll tell the teacher!"

"TEACHER!"

I am already on the scene because I am aware that I will be needed. I say, "What's happening here?"

Both talk at once: "I had it first!" "It's mine! I was playing with it!"

I speak matter-of-factly: "I see you both want the same toy."

They start to punch each other. I prevent that, and say, "I see you're both pretty angry."

"Yeah, I hate him!"

I say, "Tell him how angry you are with him."

"I feel like beating him up!"

I suggest, "Talk to him, not to me."

He turns to the other child, but before he can speak, he is answered.

"Yeah? Just try beating me up!" Both stand with clenched fists. I remain silent but ready to prevent violence.

One turns to me again. "I had it first."

"Tell him, not me."

"I had it first."

"Yeah, but it's mine. Teacher!" He appeals to me for help.

"Tell him, not me."

"I heard him. It's yours. So what?"

"So give it to me."

"You weren't even playing with it. You were drawing."

"Yeah, but now I want it."

"But why can't I play with it while you're drawing and then you can play with it?"

23

Reluctantly: "What if you wreck it?"

"I'll play here so you can watch me."

Reluctantly again: "Well, okay..."

❋❋❋❋❋❋❋❋❋❋

Encourage arguments; don't avoid them.

The lesson I learned at preschool was: "Encourage arguments; don't avoid them." The second argument took a lot longer than the first, but the extra time was well worth it. Violence was a possibility as they got more emotional about the issue, but my presence ensured that violence would not occur.

This situation is a contrast to the first argument when I was Mom. My kids' argument never got violent because they got me involved. If they needed threats of violence, they could depend on me! When they were serious about hitting each other, they didn't involve me.

The best part about the second argument is that the boys discovered their own solution. Although they dragged me into it, they did talk to each other. After a number of arguments such as this one, children learn to deal with the person in question rather than the person in charge.

Did I take this approach home and use it once I had learned it? I'm Dragon Mom, remember. Can you imagine a big monster standing quietly to one side, facilitating a problem-solving session? I continued my heavy-handed approach to settling arguments for years after I had learned better methods. And if my family punches the right buttons, they can still get Dragon Mom to come out with her wild ways and yell, scream, and put on a show over some dumb little issue.

It takes so long to change because the patterns learned in childhood are deeply ingrained. My family hid all argumentative feelings

24

because it wasn't nice to argue. When you couldn't stand it any more, you blew up. One explosion almost always caused another, and soon there would be a nasty fight. In the background of this ruckus was always my mother's quivering voice, repeating, "Let's all just be happy!"

These blowups usually ended with a self-chosen loser sulking off to pout, muttering something like, "Don't worry about me. I don't matter anyway." I don't know what anybody else did during their pouting periods, but I played little games in my head. My favorite was, "When I die, they'll be sorry!"

I'm not sure what I thought was going to kill me, but it was a beautiful picture: me on a funeral bier like Snow White and all the people who had done me wrong gathered around weeping. The fact that as a dead person I wouldn't be able to see or hear all this delicious suffering didn't bother me at all. I could still glory in the preview.

As I grew older, the picture wasn't so clear any more, but the part of me that is built around sacrifice grew into a fully-developed martyr. I would have been great on an Aztec pyramid having my still-beating heart cut from my living body. Glory! But since I was born in the wrong time and place, all I could do was suffer quietly and hope others would notice the pain engulfing me. I learned my early lessons well.

As I grew to understand myself better, I discovered that this martyr is a grown-up poor little Pitiful Precious. She is an unhealthy distortion of a part of me that should be both useful and healthy. My sacrificial self can willingly put the needs of others before her own, an important skill if not carried to extremes.

This self-sacrificing part of me really came into her own when I began having babies. I accepted the need to sacrifice a good deal of my time, interests, and even needs to care for my babies. I wasn't a martyr about it; at least, I didn't seem to need attention from others in return for the sacrifices I was making.

25

My martyr self seldom appears any more. When she was at her best, she often showed up when children were arguing, which is particularly useless, since young children couldn't care less if an adult is being martyred or not. Sacrificial moms are usually quiet in their suffering, using only the tone of voice to indicate that this is a martyr speaking, not just a plain mom with a headache. Here is an example:

✳✳✳✳✳✳✳✳✳✳

"Stop bugging me!" complains kid.

"I can't help it. I'm just singing," retorts second kid.

"MOM! He's driving me crazy!"

Martyr Mom arrives on the scene. "Children, please stop arguing! You're giving me a headache," spoken in a pleading, pitiful tone that is totally unheard.

"He keeps bugging me!"

"I'm not doing anything. He's being mean!"

"I am not!"

Mom clutches head, "Please!"

"Just make him shut up!"

"Children, my head is pounding!"

"He made a face at me!"

✳✳✳✳✳✳✳✳✳✳

Depending on how large a dose of suffering I needed, I'd eventually grit my teeth and leave the room. Sometimes the fight would escalate, so I'd go back for another dose. It seems strange to me that I continued this pattern long after I had learned other ways to handle arguments. And I still don't handle arguments at home as well as those at school. I know how to be a competent facilitator, but Martyr Mom or the dragon often take over.

Dragon Mom and Quality Time

Quality time is what makes those of us who don't spend most of our waking hours with our children feel better. We know that quality time is what counts–those shared experiences when we really focus on our children. What you may not know is that quality time doesn't have to be a "happy hour" when parent and child have fun together. Any kind of shared experience can qualify if the parent is truly attentive to the child. At the end of a long day, when you can finally spend time with your four-year-old, you may both be more in the mood to argue than to play. Arguing counts as quality time. An argument is person-to-person contact of the kind that builds a relationship. After all, that's the purpose of quality time.

The identities in the following example have been hidden to protect me from my children's wrath. You'll see that I finally learned how to take the problem-solving approach home.

❋❋❋❋❋❋❋❋❋❋

The setting is the day after Thanksgiving. Family members still at home after the celebration are sitting around the breakfast table. We are trying to decide what to do for the day–never an easy decision in this household of so many varied interests and necessities.

"Let's do something together today–like Christmas shopping and then a movie. I want to make it a family day." This suggestion comes from one young adult career person home for the holiday.

"Shopping!" groans another, an engineering student also home for three days. "I have to work on my lab problem for school next week. I'll go to the movies, though..."

"Yeah!" shouts the nine-year-old. "I want to go to the movies and take Paul!"

"No!" says the first young adult firmly. "No friends. This is a family event. Your friends bug me!"

28

"Then I don't want to go!"

"Forget it then. I'll just go to the movies on my own and go shopping by myself. The heck with all of you." The young adult starts to leave. I am stricken. My own martyr is appearing in one of my offspring!

"Be quiet, all of you! I'm sick of this!" Here comes Dragon Mom. "All you ever do is fight, fight, fight! I don't see why you always have to be so...." The dragon is on the verge of ripping into each person with insults when Janet Competent Parent takes over to facilitate.

My voice changes midsentence as the mediation approach kicks in. No one else seems to notice the switch. They're all too busy with their own feelings. I say calmly, "It's important that everyone gets a chance to talk."

I turn to the father figure, who looks like he wants to leave, except that he hasn't finished his breakfast. "What do you want to do?"

He looks uncomfortable. "I have some things to do here, and it's too crowded today for me to enjoy shopping, but I'll do whatever everyone decides." He states his opinions mildly, without whining. He doesn't sound like a martyr. I knew he was preparing for a ski trip and that he wanted to discuss the lab problem with the student engineer. He had mentioned it the night before, and I saw his calculator peeking out from under his napkin.

"I want to go to the movies and I want Paul!" the nine-year-old reminds us in an argumentative tone.

"Well, you can't have Paul or I won't go, and that's that!" The speaker gets up to leave as if the final word had been spoken.

I am calm but firm. "Just a minute. You two need to talk more about that. You each need to explain your point of view." I am feeling really proud of myself for helping them work this out instead of letting it end with neither of my children feeling heard or satisfied.

✳✳✳✳✳✳✳✳✳

29

The discussion took another half an hour, and the dragon woke up periodically, but the end result was a mutually agreeable plan that included everyone's desires, although some had to compromise. My mediation was a success. I wish I could always interrupt Dragon Mom and switch gears before I have to apologize and care for the wounded!

Over the years, I have learned some things about how to help people argue without getting emotional myself. I've never achieved perfection, and there is a gap between what I know and what I do, but I try to follow the following five principles .

How I Help My Children Argue Effectively

1. I get the arguing parties to talk to each other rather than to the person in charge.

2. I stay with the arguing parties until some resolution is achieved. This may take a long time. Even without a resolution, most arguments lose their strength if I can just stay there and keep them going until they are talked out. It requires lots of patience to do this, but the peace afterwards is well worth it.

3. I recognize that arguments are often about something other than what they seem to be about. Some arguments are purely for the purpose of catching my attention so I'll stop whatever else I'm doing. In this case, I need to ignore the argument.

4. I help both parties be honest with each other. Expression of feelings is an important part of the process of learning to argue effectively. I have discovered what I can say that will help feelings to come out. Sometimes I just state my impression of what the feelings are, but other times this approach is offensive. Sometimes just listening intently is the key.

5. I am aware of insults that hurt. When name-calling or put-downs occur, I restate what is expressed in terms of feelings. I try to do this matter-of-factly and without fuss so that I don't get emotionally involved and lose my effectiveness as a facilitator. If the child says, "You're so stupid!" I translate it to, "You're really upset about what she did."

It's never been easy for me to distinguish between arguments that are mine and those that belong solely to my children. It's easy for me to get emotionally involved even if the issue has nothing to do with me. But once I become part of the argument, I can no longer function as a facilitator.

Of course, sometimes it is appropriate for me to be emotionally involved. Sometimes I am an arguer, not a facilitator. When I'm Janet Competent Parent, I model the five principles. As an arguing party, here is what I try to do:

How I Argue Effectively

1. I stay in the argument with the person in conflict, rather than appealing to someone else.

2. I stay with the argument until it is resolved rather than stalking off to pout or stew.

3. I recognize that the topic of the argument may not be the real bone of contention. I try to remember to ask: "What's this really about?" Sometimes I ask that question of myself and the answer surprises me.

4. I try to be honest about feelings.

5. I state feelings about the action rather than criticizing the other person.

I don't always avoid taking the dragon stance by using these techniques. Sometimes I can still be seen switching my tail, breathing fire, and baring my teeth. I often hear people say it's important that children never see their parents fight. I say, "Baloney!" How are children going to learn to fight if they never see their parents fight, if things are always worked out behind their backs, or never worked out at all?

My advice is this: learn to fight fair and teach your children. Prolong arguments instead of extinguishing them. Distinguish between productive arguments and bickering designed to attract attention.

31

You have choices when in or near an argument. You can take a power stance like Dragon Mom, or you can approach the situation as a facilitator and problem-solver. If it's not your fight, you can be a mediator and keep your own feelings out of it. If it is your fight, you need to be aware of your feelings while making your choices. And, of course, if you have a dragon inside you, expect the appearance of the monster even when you're most determined to behave calmly and rationally. And love the dragon anyway!

What I know:	Periodic feelings of rejection are part of any relationship, and they are magnified in the parent-child relationship as the child grows up.
What I do:	I suffer and get hurt.
Why:	Knowing and feeling are two different things.

CHAPTER FOUR
REJECTION

Rejection is nothing new to me; I'm a writer. It's also a familiar experience for me the parent. I don't like the feeling, but I'm learning not to fear it.

I remember the time I held my first screaming newborn in my arms. His scrunched-up face, flailing fists, and stiff little body all were saying, "Rejection! Rejection!" to me. Looking back, I can see the tiny baby had no intentions of rejecting me; he was reacting to some inner need. The message came from inside me, not from him. Nevertheless, my feelings were very real–and terrifying.

I can still call forth the panic I felt as the thought crossed my mind, "What if he doesn't stop crying!?" In a rational state, even a beginner parent knows that no baby cries forever, and that the parent's job is not to make him stop, but to meet his needs. But as I held my first screaming newborn, I was far from rational.

Newborns don't intentionally reject us; they don't do anything intentionally. They are not well enough developed to think out purposes for their actions. However, they soon develop intentionality, and then the rejection is real. I remember the first time I experienced that kind of rejection, too.

My firstborn was an eager eater and I enjoyed putting the spoon into his waiting mouth. One day he was wolfing down cereal when suddenly he clamped his mouth shut and moved his face to one side. I was astonished and took the gesture very personally. He wasn't rejecting the cereal; it was me! "He doesn't love me," I said to myself. I stopped feeding him, put him down and went off upset. I didn't see at the time how ridiculous it was to be bothered because he didn't want another bite.

> *Learning to say no is important to toddler development.*

This experience was good preparation for the toddler years, when rejection became a way of life. I finally began to acquire some immunity, and even learned to laugh at myself a little. Nowadays I'm great at standing in front of a defiant toddler who is screaming, "No! No! No!" at me. I know that it's an important part of developing the personality; it's the way a child establishes himself as an individual. I no longer have a personal response to toddler rejection.

But, of course, I didn't start out calm. I used to turn into Dragon Mom and get mad.

✹✹✹✹✹✹✹✹✹

"It's time for your bath," I say sweetly.

"No!" screams my son.

"Don't you tell me no, Mister!" I make a grab for him.

He escapes from my hands and runs off, yelling, "No! No!" I can almost hear him say, "Nyah, nyah, can't catch me!" But he doesn't have enough vocabulary yet.

I run after him. He heads for the bedroom and shakes the crib. The baby wakes up crying. I stop to comfort the baby, then take up the chase again. The child is gone!

A brief search finally reveals him sitting on the coffee table contentedly eating jam out of a jar with his hands. I grab his jam-smeared body—no words this time. Tight-lipped, I carry him kicking and screaming straight to the bathroom. I'm too furious to talk.

When I finally have him in the tub, I try to tell him how angry I am. But I look down at him happily splashing, and realize that the scene is over. Only my feelings and the mess on the coffee table still remain. I watch him play until my heart rate returns to normal. Then I kneel by the tub, washcloth and soap in hand.

"No!" he screams, and the whole thing begins again.

❋❋❋❋❋❋❋❋❋❋

I get exhausted just writing about it. And to think I went through the toddler period five times! I only lived through it because somewhere along the line, I got an attitude adjustment. I came to see such defiance in a different light.

Over time, I learned to appreciate "No's." Defiance is a way to experience our own power and to express separateness—our individuality. We all have to learn to say no; it's an important part of taking care of our own needs and protecting ourselves. Once I realized that "no's" have an important function, I could then imagine that same stiff little toddler body growing up to say "No!" with the same emphasis when pressured to buy drugs or steal a car.

"No," is a perfectly good word. Once children learn to say it in the early years, they practice it over and over. When I began to think of defiance as practice rather than as personal rejection, it helped me to accept it.

> *A toddler's defiant attitude can be good practice for expressing individuality.*

Not all rejection is a result of defiance. I remember feeling most rejected on my oldest son's first day of kindergarten. Though that day marked the first significant separation of our lives together, we were both looking forward to it. I hadn't anticipated that saying goodbye would be traumatic for me.

We were both excited as we walked hand in hand up the walk to the classroom door. Other parents and children were milling around, looking in the windows, and chattering. When the bell rang, the teacher stepped outside and greeted everyone pleasantly. Before I realized it, the children had all been herded inside, my son willingly swept along with the others.

I suddenly felt terribly alone. I'll never forget the sound of the door closing behind my child. I looked at that heavy metal barrier between me and my son for a long time before I turned slowly toward the street. I felt completely shut out. I had waited for years for this day, and now that it was here, I was miserable.

More was to come. My precious son, who had previously resisted separation from his mother, not only did well on his first day but liked it! On the walk home, he bubbled about all that he had done. He talked most about the field trip that the class would take that fall—a train ride. I felt jealous.

The next blow came when a slip arrived home asking for parents to accompany the field trip. I was thrilled. I now had a way to get inside that metal door separating me from my son's classroom experiences. I happily filled out the form and stuck it in an envelope with the teacher's name on the front. Then I informed my son, "I'm going on the train ride with you!"

His face fell to his knees. "Do you have to?" he asked.

"Well, no," I answered slowly. "But," I added brightly, "I want to!"

"Oh, Mommy. Don't!" His tone was emphatic.

I was crushed. I took this rejection very seriously, and didn't go on the trip. Intellectually, I knew that separating from parents is a necessary part of growing up—that my little boy was doing exactly what he

36

needed to do. But my intellect didn't help my feelings at all.

Dragon Mom's brain is just a small part of her. Her enormous muscles are made up of "feeling fibers," each of which aches regularly as her children take the steps they need to in order to grow up.

I had more to deal with than personal rejection; I also suffered when my children were rejected.

✳✳✳✳✳✳✳✳✳✳

I'll never forget the time I stood in front of the candy counter with my three-year-old son and two-year-old daughter. I wanted to buy my mother a box of Mother's Day chocolates. My children were very interested in what was behind the glass.

As the salesperson waited on me, she caught sight of my daughter eagerly looking at a pile of chocolates at her eye level. I'm not sure what attracted the salesperson, but before I could respond, she rushed around the counter, scooped my daughter into her arms, and took her to the business side of the display case.

"Oh, you little cutie!" she gushed. "What a darling little dress that is! What piece of candy would you like? You can have any one you want. Go ahead and choose!"

From the far side of the counter, my dejected son asked, "What about me?"

Ignoring him, the salesperson went on. "How about this one? Do you like the pink one or would you rather have white?"

My son gave up. A big tear rolled down his cheek and he turned to go stand by the door. I cringe even now thinking about it. No one thought he was cute, picked him up, or offered him a piece of candy. I tried to make it up to him by letting him choose a piece, but candy wasn't the issue. We both felt the pain of his rejection.

✳✳✳✳✳✳✳✳✳✳

I still don't take rejection easily, mine or my children's. But even with my small dragon brain I have begun to separate different types of rejections. For example, I have learned to separate personal rejection from the kind which doesn't have anything to do with me. Most of the rejection I feel from my children is because I'm their parent. It has nothing to do with me personally. I know that I am not being rejected with my son's breakfast cereal. I know too that toddlers shouting, "No!" are only establishing self-assertion. I should feel pleased that our relationship is such that they are able even now to defy and resist me. Sitting here at the computer, it's easy to say so. But just let one of my children push me away, which they now do symbolically rather than physically, and I still get upset. I don't like to feel rejected, and I guess that won't ever change.

✳✳✳✳✳✳✳✳✳✳

Tim's worries began the week before he started school, at kindergarten orientation. Although Tim had been to preschool, kindergarten was scary to him. He clung to me throughout orientation. When the children were asked to sit on the floor in front of their parents, he stayed glued to my lap. When the teacher took the children outside to tour the school grounds, Tim refused to leave the room without me.

The face of Tim's teacher registered her disapproval. Afterward, I started a conversation with Tim's teacher. I explained that I would walk in with him on the first day and stay until he was comfortable. She interrupted me firmly. "No parents allowed!" She stated the rule as if it had been written in stone by the hand of God. She made it clear in three words that kindergarten was a parent-free zone.

That's when Tim's stomachaches started. There were four days of worry until the big day. We had a talk. I asked him, "What will you do?"

"About what?"

"About going to school for the first time by yourself."

He thought about it before he came up with an answer. "I'll say goodbye to you at the door, then I'll walk in and get under the table."

The day arrived, and Tim said goodbye at the door and walked into the classroom. At noon, I stood outside the door waiting for him. Children streamed out, chattering excitedly. I overheard one girl tell her mother, "There was this kid hiding, and I said to the teacher, 'Look! There's a kid under the table!' and everybody laughed."

I was in agony with the pain my son must have felt. I was surprised to see him come skipping out cheerfully.

"Well," I asked him. "What happened?"

"What do you mean?" he asked.

"This morning. When you first got there."

He still didn't seem to know what I was talking about until I mentioned his plan. "Oh, I went under the table and a girl told the teacher and everybody laughed. The teacher told me to come out, so I did." That was the end of the conversation. He never mentioned the incident again.

✳✳✳✳✳✳✳✳✳✳

What I know:	There are good techniques to get kids to clean up messes.
What I do:	Sometimes I just ignore messes. More often, I expect my children to pick up after themselves without being told, or with a simple reminder. When they don't, I get mad and pick up myself. Sometimes I think I'm mad at my children because they're so messy, when it's really my ineffectiveness that makes me unhappy.
Why:	Sometimes it's more trouble than it's worth to pick up messes. Sometimes I don't feel like confronting or even interacting. Sometimes I worry that I will inhibit them from creative activities if I make them clean up. Sometimes I'm too laid back to worry about it. Sometimes I have other priorities. (I can hear my mother's voice: "Sometimes you're just too lazy!")

CHAPTER FIVE
MESSES

Messes are a big part of my life. As a person who chose to have five children, I have to say that I chose messes. You must think I'm out of my mind!

When I became a preschool teacher, I learned that it is important for young children to have sensory experiences–translated into everyday language, that means to make messes. I used to allow and even encourage glorious messes at school–like body painting and mud play.

I remember the time one child discovered he could paint by hitting the brush against his hand and creating spatters on his paper. I was aware that the spatters were going beyond the paper, but he was in such a creative mode that I didn't stop him. What a mess we had to clean up afterward! But it wasn't a problem; he helped, other kids helped, and I remained cheerful. The only problem with messes at preschool came from parents who got stuffy about paint on clothes.

> *Messes don't always bring out Dragon Mom.*

Now I suppose you expect me to say that messes at home trigger Dragon Mom, causing her to go into a frenzied display of anger. Surprisingly, that's not always true. I love watching preschoolers, even my own, creatively dabble in sand, clay, mud, and water at home. That's one area of overlap between my teacher me and my parent me. It's interesting that my children did less of this kind of mess-making than many children—possibly because they knew it was something I wanted them to do.

Messes can be a complicated issue for adults. Making messes usually holds a lot of leftover childhood energy. Many of us conjure up childhood images of grownups having apoplexy over spilled milk, muddy floors, or strewn toys.

I remember the day I saw this condition in my husband.

✳✳✳✳✳✳✳✳✳✳

I had been having a good time at home with my three-year-old, his friend, and some goop. Goop is cornstarch and water—a wonderfully gooshy substance that acts in weird ways. Those two little boys were having a glorious sensory experience.

At first, the activity was fairly contained in a dishpan on a table. But when they really got into it, they started adding cars and toys, racing around the house to collect additional objects. Of course, as they ran they were dripping goop. Had this been any other substance, I would

42

have restricted them to the dishpan, but goop, once dry, is very easy to clean up. The powdery cornstarch brushes off clothes and skin and is easily vacuumed from floors and furniture.

I have to admit that I wasn't supervising the boys closely, but I was well prepared to do the cleanup once they were finished. So I left them to play. I was in the other room at the computer. The boys were in the kitchen, hall, and bedroom, spreading goop and cars.

I heard the back door open. Innocently, I walked out to see who it was. There stood my mild-mannered husband, briefcase fallen at his feet, mouth open, with a dangerous red flush rising from his collar. I'd never before seen him in that condition. He stood staring at what must have seemed to him the granddaddy of all messes. I'm sure that all the feelings and childhood messages he ever got about messes were ringing in his ears during this period of paralysis. Then he exploded.

Eventually I got all the pieces of my husband and house back together. But he was still so upset that it was difficult to discuss his feelings.

"Please promise you won't ever let them do that again," he pleaded.

"I just can't promise that." Apology was in my voice, but I meant what I said.

Instead of promising, I learned to time "sensory experiences" so that he didn't happen on them unexpectedly. I don't think he ever got over the shock of that goop scene.

✳✳✳✳✳✳✳✳✳

This story may give the impression that I'm a wonderful parent in the face of messes. Wrong. Creative messes are fine. But food messes? That's a different story. For some reason, Dragon Mom can sleep soundly during art and sensory exploration, letting Janet Competent Parent handle things. But one little cooking or eating mess

43

wakes her in an instant. Peanut butter on the tablecloth, honey on the floor, flour in the utensil drawer: it doesn't take much to get her into a frenzy.

"Why can't you be more careful with the milk!?"

"If you're going to cook with me, you'd better stop dripping that honey!"

And, finally, "Get out of here! I can't stand another minute of this!"

I have my share of issues with messes, just like my husband. All those issues came to the forefront when I became a parent.

Looking back, I can see that babies' messes were frustrating but manageable. Sure, they spit up and smeared their food and made unpleasant pastes and piles in their diapers. And their equipment was all over the house. But since they couldn't take responsibility, it was just a matter of constantly cleaning them up and wiping up or picking up after them. I remember getting mighty tired of it, but not rabid.

In fact, I have a clear memory of my early motherhood as a time of order. I felt good about that. When I had two children under three years of age in a tiny apartment, I had to be organized. I didn't have an overabundance of possessions, and I was good at getting rid of outgrown and no-longer-useful items. I had periods of thinking that cleaning and straightening up would never end, but I realize now that those tasks were manageable during that period of my life.

Those in the baby period of their parenting careers may not be able to relate to the above paragraph. One's perspective while in that time of life is quite different than when looking back on it. Some may be tearing their hair and feeling that constant messes are not at all manageable. So I certainly don't want to mention that it will get worse. It did for me, but my story is not necessarily the same as anyone else's.

When the babies got old enough to accept some responsibility, things got a lot harder for me. The peak of the mess issue hit when I had four children under the age of six in a three-bedroom house. Cleanup was very complex. There was no clear time when they were finished playing, except when we left the house or at bedtime.

And just because the children were finished playing so we could pick up doesn't mean that I was able to manage it. Conducting a cleanup session while getting ready to go out often seemed impossible. By the time the kids were ready, it was time to go. There was no time to pick up toys.

Bedtime wasn't much better. My energy was at a low ebb. Besides, if we had waited until bedtime, the mess was usually out of hand. If we had picked up earlier, it was all soon pulled out again and I had morphed into Dragon Mom—either grouchy or a raving maniac, depending on how strewn and sticky the floor was.

My usual approach was to ignore the mess as much as possible until I couldn't handle it any more, or until company was expected. To this day, if my daughter finds me in a cleanup session, she automatically asks, "Who's coming over?"

If you dropped over, my house was messy but I had an excuse. If you announced in advance that you were coming, I'd manage to get it all cleaned up. Those were the good old days. Today, I am still dealing with messes and only one child lives at home. My excuse is that I have more important things to do, but it's not as good an excuse as all those little kids were!

✳✳✳✳✳✳✳✳✳

Dragon Mom, Homemaker

Tim and I were making his father's birthday cake. As he squished eggs and dripped batter, I got more and more tense. He loved the electric mixer, and was making swirls and patterns, dotting the walls with cake batter spray. Finally, I unplugged the beater. "Hey!" I told myself through gritted teeth, "Just change to a happy channel." So I did.

"That's enough," I said kindly.

Actually, it was too much. The batter was hopelessly overbeaten. An hour later, when we tried to remove the cake from the pan, it crumbled into pieces, a chunk falling at my feet into the cat dish.

"Let's just glue it together like a puzzle," I said cheerily. We attacked the project with a big bowl of frosting. The result was pretty ugly.

I was sick of the whole domestic scene before we were finished cleaning up. I fled to my constant refuge: the computer.

When I emerged later to serve the cake, my husband gasped at the sight of it. Before we started eating, I said in sheepish voice, "I have something to show you." In my hand was a tarnished pin, inscribed, "FUTURE HOMEMAKER OF THE YEAR."

"Where did you get that?" my husband asked, his voice betraying his surprise.

"I won it in high school."

My husband looked around at the messy kitchen and the cake which looked like it had been through an earthquake.

"No kidding," he murmured. "What did you do to win it?"

I paused dramatically before responding, "I wrote an essay."

✳✳✳✳✳✳✳✳✳

I have come to look at messes from several different points of view. If I explain them, maybe I won't even need to give you excuses! I make messes myself–it's the way I work. I work best at the kitchen table, on the floor, or at the computer with materials spread out around me. And I like to work on several projects at once. In fact, while I am writing these words, I am home alone in a huge mess.

I have a nest of papers, books, and file folders from school scattered on the kitchen table. On the couch are clothes I haven't finished folding. In the front room with the computer are all the papers, notes, and folders I am using to write this chapter and get inspired about the next. In my bedroom is a stack of mail I'm planning to deal with sometime today. I'll get to most of this before the family gets home tonight, but what I don't finish, I won't put away. I'll stack it neatly, maybe, but I'll leave it out. Putting things away makes it hard to get a project going again. I also lose things when I put them away, so I resist doing it.

Recognizing my own style and needs makes me more tolerant of the unfinished projects of my children. I don't always make them put things away. I often allow block structures to remain standing–usually stretched across the living room, where there is more space. But obviously we can't all live together the way I do when I'm alone, or the chaos would be unbearable. So I confine my mess-making to times when I have the house to myself. The rest of the time, I'm more careful to confine my own clutter and keep an eye on that of other family members. I ride a fine line between relaxing and ignoring messes, or getting uptight and taking action. I choose the second alternative less because of a decision I made. It used to be that my sense of personal worth was tied to the order and cleanliness of the place I lived in. I don't know if men have those feelings, but they are common among the women I know. Even though I shared the home with the rest of the family, I took full responsibility for its condition. I felt that it was my job to either see that the

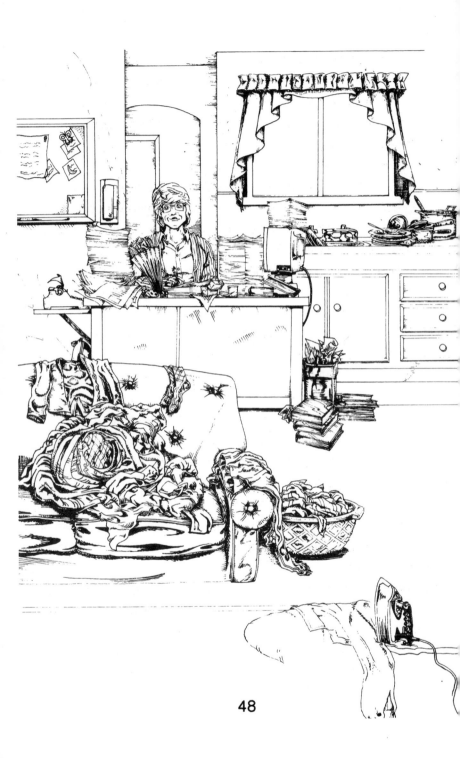

place was picked up by those who had made the messes, or to do it myself. If I didn't do either, I felt uncomfortable, angry, judged by others, and upset with myself. As a result, I lived in a much more organized and sanitary environment than I do now. However, I didn't have as full and productive a life during that period of order.

Then one day I realized two things:

1. I didn't have to take full responsibility. The condition of a home ought to be the joint responsibility of those who live in it.
2. I couldn't be a parent, teacher, writer, wife, and person and continue to do all the housecleaning.

Dragon Mom had never been very effective at getting cooperation from others. Mrs. Bodunky usually emerged and did it all herself. So I traded housekeeping for writing, and life has been better since. This change does not mean that I don't feel responsibility for my share, or that I don't get upset when others don't hold up their end. But I did unhook my sense of worth from the condition of my home.

If someone drops by and catches us in a mess, my apologies may sound the same these days, but they don't feel the same. I'm only apologizing for myself; I'm not taking responsibility for the others. And my apologies no longer contain the feeling that I'm worth less because I've allowed a mess to happen.

Some people require a greater degree of order and cleanliness than I do, and some people need less. Some people get pleasure out of cleaning. Some find it even more odious than I do. But I'm glad that I've examined my own priorities and made some conscious decisions. What about children? Don't they need to learn to be orderly? Doesn't a parent have the responsibility to teach them organization and tidiness? My answer is this: what you teach and what they learn are likely to be completely different. I remember friends in college who, after eighteen years of neatness lessons at home, became total slobs at college when no one was standing over them. Other people come from messy homes, yet seem to have an inherent need for order. They create islands of order wherever they are, even if no one else around them cares in the least. The way you are raised doesn't necessarily determine how you will live when you have choices.

I don't mean to give the impression that there is no hope, so you might just as well give up and drown in children's messes. Of course Janet the expert has some advice. But if the advice doesn't work, and your children grow up to behave differently than you planned, do reconsider the complexity of the issue and love yourself anyway.

Advice #1:　　Remember the old adage, and practice what you preach. If you're sitting in your own mess watching soaps on television, you're dead in the water if you yell into the other room, "Get that mess in there picked up!" Modeling is a powerful teacher. Children are likely to imitate adults. If you pick up behind yourself, there's a chance that they will. Of course, if you go too far in the other direction, the old rebellion rule may come into play. Some children, rather than imitate their messy parents, decide to do the opposite. But if you really want your children to grow up with a sense of order, it's safer to try modeling than depend on rebellion.

Advice #2:　　Make cleanup time fun–or at least matter-of-fact. Avoid any hints that this is something they shouldn't want to do. Dragon Mom is not good at this one: "Pick up those toys this minute!" Little children don't even know that picking up is an unpleasant chore unless you somehow give them that message. The adult attitude makes a big difference. Toddlers delight in dumping things. They also delight in refilling. Instead of yelling at them for dumping, the trick is to suggest that they put the stuff back in. Demonstrate when necessary,and when the container is full, take it away before the next dumping.

Advice #3:　　Avoid the power struggle by taking a problem-solving and teamwork approach. Don't just issue orders; get physically involved. "I'll pick up the long blocks; you pick up the square ones." Choosing between a cooperative attitude and a power stance can make all the difference in the world.

Advice #4:   Try to schedule something desirable for the next event after pickup time. "We can go for our walk as soon as the room is picked up." It's a lot harder to get things in order if the next event is going to be getting a shot at the doctor's.

Advice #5:   Provide a fairly high degree of order in the environment for young children. They need you to sort and arrange their toys and possessions - they can't do it for themselves. They <u>can</u> put things away easily when there is a place for each item. This kind of start gives them a feeling of security and predictability, which can carry over into later years as a sense of organization.

After you give your children a good start by being somewhat organized and orderly, it's time to turn responsibility for their space and possessions over to them. It's also time to decide how to handle joint responsibility for shared living areas. A first step in this process is examining closely what degree of order is right for you. The next step is to find ways to live agreeably with those who are more or less orderly than you are.

Most of the time, this whole process in families takes place on an unconscious level, and results in a good number of ugly arguments, hurt feelings, and power struggles. You can't expect to completely avoid power struggles and bad feelings, but it may help to understand what they are really about. It also helps if you're clear about responsibility, which is the subject of the next chapter.

Clutter can Lead to Buried Treasure

"One of the advantages of being disorderly is that one is constantly making exciting discoveries," said A.A. Milne, creator of Winnie the Pooh and Christopher Robin.

It's true! If I didn't have messes lying around to sort out, I wouldn't find wonderfully serendipitous things that have great meaning for me. The surprises I encounter when sorting things are a lot like buried treasure found when weeding the garden. If I were orderly, I would throw away things—never realizing that they might become precious later.

What I know:	Children need to learn to be responsible for themselves.
What I do:	I take responsibility away from children.
Why:	The dragon-Bodunky pattern is a way of life for me!

CHAPTER SIX
RESPONSIBILITY

A common way to teach responsibility is to buy the child a pet. The pattern is very familiar to me. I've given in more than once during a conversation like the following:

❋❋❋❋❋❋❋❋❋❋

"I want a hamster."

"Well, you'd have to take care of it."

"I will."

"I don't know if it's such a good idea. Maybe you'd get tired of it."

"I won't! I won't! I know I won't! PLEASE...."

"I don't know..."

"I'll be good for the rest of my life if you'll just buy it!"

"Well, I guess it would teach you some responsibility."

"Oh, thank you, thank you!" (hug, hug, kiss, kiss.)

Hamster arrives complete with fifty-dollar cage. Child is good for about fifteen minutes. Child is interested in hamster for anywhere from a few hours to a few weeks. Child loses interest. Feeding pet becomes an unbearable chore. Parent takes over care and feeding. End of responsibility lesson.

❋❋❋❋❋❋❋❋❋❋

Buying a pet is not the best way to teach responsibility for the simple reason that children can't experience the consequences of their acts. If a child agrees to do something but does not live up to the agreement, the parent should allow the child to find out what happens as a result. Obviously, one cannot allow an innocent animal to die for a lesson.

One alternative would be what's called a logical consequence, such as giving the animal away. That response would teach the lesson. But many parents are like me, Dragon Mom-Bodunky, and get very angry –just before they take the responsibility upon themselves.

The arguments I use to keep from giving away the pet are fuzzy ones. "He'll never forgive me if I give his pet away." "Giving away his hamster intrudes on his private rights." But then, most of the arguments I use when parenting are somewhat fuzzy. As Dragon Mom and Mrs. Bodunky, I act from my gut mostly, not from my head. Janet Competent Parent is the only one of us who acts appropriately from both gut and head. Unfortunately, she's a rare visitor to my home.

Teaching responsibility was always a serious goal for me, as it is for most parents. My vision of my grownup children was of fully responsible adults. I know that the best way to reach this goal is by letting children experience the consequences of their acts.

Children need to experience the consequences of their acts.

Bedrooms are a good example. I have always believed that the private space each person occupies is his or her responsibility from early on. During the toddler and preschool years, I took responsibility for arranging my children's space in such a way that they could manage it. I organized their toys: I had a place for each, I carried away the worn-out or outgrown toys, I kept back some so that there weren't overwhelming numbers to deal with.

I also decorated their rooms and play areas attractively. At several points I even labelled shelves in the best preschool tradition so that pickup was easy. They even got some intellectual stimulation from matching toys to words. But by the time they were ready for elementary school, I backed off, leaving each fully responsible for his or her own space. With shared bedrooms, that meant some negotiations and lots of arguments. There's nothing wrong with that. I didn't pick up, and I wasn't very good about helping find lost articles in a messy bedroom, either. I was good about shutting doors when company came, and I still am.

Responsibility for shared living space is another matter. Methods for assigning chores fill parenting books. Since I'm not so good at it, I'll just give it a light once-over. As I mentioned, I believe in shared responsibility. What happens if the rest of the family doesn't? Well, then you use a problem-solving approach, which includes expressing feelings, brainstorming, negotiation, compromise, making a plan, executing the plan, and evaluating. There are plenty of available books on this process.

I'm not saying it doesn't work, because it does. I am saying that many parents, including me, don't use it very often. My usual pattern concerning chores is the Dragon Mom-Bodunky approach.

❋❋❋❋❋❋❋❋❋❋

Step One: We reach some kind of agreement on what will be done by whom. Part of the agreement usually includes the consequences for not following through. Then the agreement is followed for awhile. Sometimes I skip step one and just assign the job, which almost guarantees that step two of the pattern will commence

55

immediately.

Step Two: The child in question neglects the chore.

Step Three: I confront the child. "Hey, I see that the trash isn't emptied yet."

"Yeah, Mom. I'm gonna do it."

"When?"

"Soon's I finish this." The child is on his stomach on the floor playing a never-ending video game.

Pause. Repeat Step Three.

Step Three is sometimes repeated as many as five times.

Step Four: Dragon Mom arrives. "If you don't take out that trash right now, you're going to be very sorry!" Realizing that general threats are weak, Dragon Mom gets specific. "I'm going to throw away that dumb video game, keep you home from the movies for six months, and put you on restriction for the rest of your life!"

Child remains unmoved on the floor, hand on the controls.

"Will you listen to me!?" Dragon Mom is screaming now, jumping up and down. The room trembles, but the child continues to twiddle the controls.

"I'm losing control!" gasps Dragon Mom, running out into the fresh air.

Moments later, the door opens and here comes dear, sweet Mrs. Bodunky, wearing a fresh white apron and smelling of talcum powder. Stepping over the child and video game, Bodunky moves smoothly across the room, trailing marshmallow cream in her wake. The child swipes one finger across the wake and sticks it in his mouth. Smiles contentedly.

In the meantime, Mrs. Bodunky, ever efficient, has emptied the trash, cleaned out the bottom of the wastebasket with a rag, and put in a fresh bag. She is humming to herself. The child continues playing

Nintendo. He is smiling to himself. End of pattern.

❋❋❋❋❋❋❋❋❋❋

Strange, that with all my parenting experience and education, I've just never been any good at getting a child to empty the trash–or do most other little chores. That last scene demonstrates why. The child had no motivation to empty the trash and I never provided any. I just bugged him until I felt powerless, then got angry.

However, ineffective as I am, my children somehow learned trash-emptying skills. Four of my five children now live in places of their own, and not one of them lives with an exceptional number of unemptied wastebaskets. Of course, since Bodunky doesn't come over to help them out, they have some motivation. Overflowing, smelly trash in your home can be very compelling.

I'm glad that my children seem to have learned these little responsibilities in spite of my failure to teach them. I haven't been such a failure in other areas of responsibility, such as schoolwork. That is a responsibility I completely leave to my children, and mostly it has worked quite well, saving me a lot of ulcers.

> *Schoolwork is the responsibility of the child.*

The way I see it, my children's schoolwork and grades are their responsibility. My responsibility is to provide them with proper nourishment, rest, and exercise. I never did get around to supplying each with a place to study, let alone a desk of his or her own, but they were quite creative in finding places for themselves. I never suggested places to study or saw to it that they sat down to do their work.

> **Dragon Mom Passes Breakfast Test**
>
> You know those days when the teacher asks the class to write down what they had for breakfast? In my fantasy, the teacher keeps a file folder on each parent. The day of the "breakfast test," the teacher gives a grade and puts it in that folder. Since parents never see their own "report cards," they can only speculate about the teacher's evaluation.
>
> Well, I know I always passed the breakfast test because I made my kids eat a hearty breakfast before school. I stuffed protein down them even though they regularly had stomach aches when they got to school.
>
> That's okay. I was only being graded on breakfast content, not on stomach aches. I'm happy to say that they eventually outgrew the pain. I only hope that the teachers really did ask them--at least once--what they ate for breakfast!

I did not monitor school assignments or make children sit down for a certain time each day. I always figured they'd had enough of that during school. As a result, each child developed his or her own study habits and ways of meeting deadlines. They also suffered the consequences of their actions when they failed to take responsibility. This approach usually worked well because the consequences teachers thought up were sufficient to motivate my children. That may not be true for all children.

I did not expect all my children to be A students, and I did not push them to excel in school. I figured each, left alone, would make his or her own decision about the importance of grades. And they did. Instead of insisting they all go to college, I encouraged them to discover for themselves how they wanted to support themselves. What they chose determined whether they needed to go to college. As it turned out, all of them have at least tried college, except the youngest, who is still in high school. Modeling is at work here, since most of the family in my generation and some of the previous generation are college graduates.

I have been criticized for my attitude toward grades, especially by my children. I've been informed more than once that other kids got paid for A's. But my attitude is that their grades are my children's business, not mine. I don't pay for A's or punish for F's. I don't ignore my children's feelings about their grades. I cheer or commiserate, but I try to make my reaction a reflection of their feelings, not my own.

Rather than "I'm proud of you," I try to say, "You must be very proud of yourself for earning that A!" "I guess you're pretty unhappy about that F," works better for me than "I'm disappointed about that F."

I learned early on that grades mean different things to different people, and I try to respect that. I remember one elementary school open house where I was surprised to see a book report star chart with no stars next to my son's name. Since this son read constantly, I asked him about the lack of stars. "Oh," he said matter-of-factly, "I don't need stars to make me read." He obviously understood that the chart was designed to motivate, and he didn't need recognition or competition to motivate him.

Later, when this same son decided he wanted to attend a prestigious university, he changed his mind about grades and recognition. He went to work on his grades, and did very well. Not all my children made the same decision, so the grade point averages in my family are widely diverse.

I don't take responsibility for my children's successes–academic or other kinds. By the same token, I don't take responsibility for their failures. Of course I cheer, and sometimes cry, along with them. But I try to separate their successes and failures from my own. I also try hard to perceive how they respond to success and failure–how they label and define the events in their lives. What I consider successes and failures don't always look the same to them.

It seems strange to me that I am able to turn big responsibilities and life decisions over to my children, but unable to do the same thing with little ones like taking out the trash. I must admit that giving children responsibility to the extent that I do, except for chores, is a different approach from that of many parents. I remember once when a son complained mightily about it.

"Mom, I hate it when you make me decide things for myself. My friends' parents just say, 'Do this, do that..' Then the kid can decide not to do it, and if he gets caught, he just gets punished. But once it's over, it's over. He doesn't have to think about it anymore until the next time he decides not to do it. I think that's a better way to raise kids!"

That's what he said when he was fourteen. When he was twenty, he said, "I really like the way you let me have responsibility for myself and my decisions. It was hard sometimes, but I think I'm a better person for it."

Not that he gave up trying to get me to be responsible. I remember the time he called from college: "Can I buy a motorcycle?"

I said, "Why are you asking me? You're over eighteen; it's your money. You know I feel very strongly that they are dangerous and I hate the thought of you riding one in traffic."

That response was enough to launch him into the merits of motorcycles. You'd have thought I had told him he couldn't have one. When he finished, I repeated my negative feelings and handed the responsibility for the decision back to him. He really wanted to be a little boy again and be told that he wasn't old enough to decide. But it wasn't true, and we both knew it. Perhaps he wanted to be able to blame me if he got a motorcycle and ended up in an accident. But I refused to make the decision, and I wouldn't take the blame. I did tell him my point of view.

Of course I protected my children when they needed it. I didn't suddenly begin when they were teenagers to give them full responsibility for their own welfare. Instead, I started to allow risk-taking early on, carefully weighing the degree of risk. I let them climb things, but not high enough to get hurt if they fell. They learned to make decisions about what was dangerous, which is an important process if a child is to grow into a responsible teenager. As children, they need the kind of risks where failure teaches but doesn't damage, where the value of the lesson outweighs the pain of the consequences. If risk-taking is graduated as they grow older, children develop decision-making skills. By the teen years, when they must deal with decisions where the stakes are higher, like drugs and sex, they are more capable of making judgments.

There is another aspect of responsibility. Consider these statements:

"It's not my fault! He made me do it!'

"You make me so mad!"

"You're driving me crazy!"

These common statements reflect a lack of responsibility for acts and feelings. I can't pretend that I've been a perfect model. I find it easy to blame my actions and my feelings on sources outside myself. Like my children.

Responsibility for feelings is the hardest one of all for me. I was brought up to explain the source of feelings outside the individual. The expression, "You make me so mad!" illustrates this phenomenon well. It's one of Dragon Mom's favorite expressions. Consider this scene:

✳✳✳✳✳✳✳✳✳✳

Child runs through front door straight into living room across newly-cleaned light beige rug. Behind him lumbers Dragon Mom, yelling and breathing fire.

"You...you...!" She stops before she says the names that come to her lips. Earlier, she would have screamed vile names at this child, slamming his character. Now she has learned not to call her children names, knowing that they stick. Even her small brain does absorb a few lessons. At a loss for words, she howls, growls, and then screams, "You make me so blankety-blank mad!" and launches into a tirade about how

61

inconsiderate the child is, how much trouble he has caused, and how he doesn't care how upset he makes her.

By this time, the child has seen his mistake and is looking back and forth between the prints on the rug and the mud on his shoes. He takes them off and departs to the other room, shoes in hand. The dragon, still jumping up and down, doesn't even see him leave. Eventually, she too departs, swinging her tail behind her, overturned furniture in her wake.

Enter Mrs. Bodunky with a bucket and scrub brush in hand. The scene ends with her on the rug beside the muddy prints, one hand over her heart. She is muttering, "That child will be the death of me! He's trying to drive me crazy!"

From the other room comes the sound of a video game, where the child in stocking feet is controlling some muscled hero fighting space monsters.

✳✳✳✳✳✳✳✳✳✳

Neither Dragon Mom nor Bodunky see themselves as the source of their own feelings. They believe the child is making them feel they way they do. They blame their unpleasant feelings on the child. They don't understand that competent parents do feel and express anger. Here's how Janet C. Parent would act if she were there:

✳✳✳✳✳✳✳✳✳✳

She stops the child in his journey across the rug, and looks straight into his eyes to say, "I just spent a lot of money to get that rug cleaned and now it's got mud on it! I feel really angry and upset." The tone of her voice is similar to the dragon's; it's obvious that she is really very angry.

She looks to see if the child has made the connection between himself and the mud on the rug. If he appears to be unaware, she makes the connection for him. "You walked into the living room with muddy

62

feet." She is careful to blame the action and not criticize the child's character. She, too, may jump up and down and even shake when she gets mad. Competent parents don't lack feelings, but they own their feelings by saying, "I feel..." rather than "You make me feel..."

After she has expressed her feelings, she makes it clear that the child has the responsibility for remedying the situation. She may provide him with instructions and materials, but he is the one who cleans up the rug–not she.

✳✳✳✳✳✳✳✳✳✳

Knowing how to act doesn't mean that I act that way. Dragon Mom doesn't spend a lot of time thinking. She just reacts, and then calls in Bodunky to relieve her guilt. But as I learn to accept the dragon in me, she is beginning to see things differently. She may never own her feelings; she just doesn't think in those terms. But she's getting better at expressing them. Sometimes she doesn't even criticize or blame when she blows up! Best of all, she may someday begin to use all that energy to guide and direct the child to correct his own mistakes, clean up his own messes, wipe up the mud. Then, when Bodunky shows up with all of her nurturing qualities, the effect will be beneficial. The two make a good team, though they are often misguided. They both need a good lesson in discipline, which brings us to the next chapter.

What I know:	There are at least eighteen effective ways to discipline without getting mad.
What I do:	I get mad.
Why:	When I get emotional, I forget what I know.

CHAPTER SEVEN
DISCIPLINE

Janet the expert really wanted to write this chapter. After all, what does Dragon Mom know about discipline? But this is the dragon's book, so let's start with what she knows. Even as a big, clumsy, pea-brained monster, I have learned something about discipline over the years. I have learned self-control.

Oh, sure, I always go farther than I intend. I'm not perfect at self-control and make no claims to be. But I know when I've stepped over the first limit line because I begin to feel guilty. I don't stop what I'm doing, but I'm aware that I don't want to be doing it. Even more important, I'm aware of the final limit line, and I stop before I go over it.

I'm not saying I've never hit my kids. As a beginner, I hit them on purpose. I believed that spanking was the way to control my children. I taught the first ones not to touch electrical outlets or run into the street by spanking them.

But as I got more experience, better models, and some education, I learned other ways to teach the same things. Once I found those other ways, I didn't have to spank any more. I was glad to quit spanking because once I had thought about it I was able to see that it didn't really accomplish my true goals. Even a dragon brain could see that if I hit my children for hitting someone else I was modeling the behavior I was trying to eliminate. My brain is small, but it can grasp bits of logic.

I also have to admit that spanking was not always purely to teach a lesson. More often, it was about expressing my anger. Even the small amounts of logic I possessed got lost when that happened. Giving up spanking as a method of behavior control took away the emotional expression aspect of it–thank goodness! Venting anger by hitting children is just too risky. It's too easy to step over the final limit line and do real damage. I'm sorry for parents who don't see this. And there are numbers of them, according to the child abuse statistics.

If you don't spank, how do you keep children out of danger, prevent them from hurting others, and keep them in line? I'm glad you asked that question. You did ask it, didn't you? Everyone does, sooner or later, when I state that I don't believe in spanking.

Well, my size and strength alone can prevent and control many of my children's behaviors. At least at first, I'm a lot bigger than they are. Of course, size by itself won't work forever, so it's important to aim at turning the outside discipline and control necessary in early childhood into self-discipline and inner control as soon as possible.

A parent's size alone can prevent unwanted behaviors.

Here's an example of how size and bulk can be used to control. Suppose I say, "I don't want you to climb on the kitchen counter. It's dangerous and I need to keep it clean." If the child doesn't readily climb down, which children almost never do, I can follow up by putting the child down on the floor. I can stand between the child and the drawers or stool he used to climb up. I can remove the child from the room if necessary. And if I use my size and bulk right away, instead of depending on words alone, the child learns that I mean what I say and am prepared to follow through. I don't have to get mad, because I can change the unacceptable behavior. Naturally, Dragon Mom forgets this and often spends time fussing, carrying on, threatening, complaining, and finally getting furious before she removes the child from the counter.

> *Controlling the environment can help to control behavior.*

Janet Competent Parent also uses the environment to control children. When they were very little, fences, gates, and locked doors told them where they couldn't go. I didn't have a rule about not touching the wood stove; I had a fence around it. Now that they are older, no one needs a fence or a rule to protect them from the heat of the stove.

The controls on the TV were a different story. If I were a cabinet designer, I'd hide the controls and put a child-proof catch on the place where I hid them. That's the environmental approach to teaching TV discipline. But since controls are often right out there, inviting little fingers to touch them, you either have to figure out ways to prevent that exploration or be willing for the child to experience and explore.

Slapping hands will work, but little children should be encouraged to touch things, not discouraged. The urge to touch is very strong during the first couple of years—and for a good reason. Touching is one of the major ways children develop their intelligence. If you destroy that urge, you can affect their brains and their attitudes. Children who are taught not to touch explore less and have a narrower range of early experiences than touchers. A wide range of early experience is important for development.

Saying "No" a million times or so creates the same problem. Besides, it gets tiresome and frustrating. And it sets up a pattern in their minds which becomes highly active as they become two and all your "no's" get returned tenfold!

Better to use your size and bulk to remove the child and give her something else to touch. With some imagination, you may be able to find some other interesting things to do. How about a board with a series of knobs and buttons? Or how about removing the TV entirely–which would be good for all of you anyway. The TV controls are inviting; that's the difficulty. They are fun to manipulate and give a sense of power. When the environment gives such a strong invitation, it's hard to resist.

Grocery stores offer other enticements. They are set up to practically beg you to take things off the shelves, which, of course, is why trips to the store with children are so difficult. Environmental messages are very strong. Children do much better when the environment says, "Touch me," and means it–the way a play yard, play room, or children's museum should do.

When the environmental messages are clear and appropriate, behavior is easy. But many environments are set up for one thing, but then used in a variety of ways. Children's bedrooms are a good example. Most are designed for stimulation. The message is, "Play! Be active; be awake!" Trying to settle down a child in a room screaming with color and alive with toys can be very difficult. Since you're not going to remodel the room twice a day, an alternative is to at least change the mood by turning down lights, making soft sounds, and otherwise providing a transition between being wide awake and going to sleep. The process would be easier in an environment designed just for sleeping.

> *When possible, provide choices.*

Giving choices is another effective way of guiding and controlling behavior. Make it clear that you won't allow unacceptable behavior, but provide a couple of alternatives. "I won't let you hit your brother, but you can hit on the pounding bench or smack this pillow." Even Dragon Mom, if she remembers, can say such simple words. And she has the size and strength to back them up when necessary.

I had accumulated a wide variety of parenting techniques by the time my youngest son came along. He had more to imitate than my other children. I'll never forget the day I picked him up from preschool, and as I buckled him into his seat, he informed me matter-of-factly, "I won't let you take me straight home. You have a choice of taking me to Jason's house to play or taking me to the store to buy a toy." My response is not part of the memory, unfortunately, but since I could drive and he couldn't, I guess we both realized it was a bluff.

> *For better or worse, modeling is the strongest influence on child behavior.*

Modeling is another method of guiding children's behavior. Spanking is ineffective precisely because children tend to imitate their parents. If you have a dragon within you, as I do, this imitation factor becomes a real problem. Your children will remind you of your dragon self by coming out with some statement or tone of voice that sounds just like you at your worst.

"If you don't stop that right now, I'm going to beat the living daylights out of you!" As a child, I used to yell and scream at my dolls. I still have my living daylights, so I know it never happened to me, but those very words that once came out of my mother also came out of my own mouth. My children have updated the vocabulary a bit, but they nevertheless model themselves after me, who followed my mother's pattern, who followed her mother, and so on.

"Want me to punch out your lights?" asks one son, taking a karate stance.

"Yeah? You and who else?" replies his brother, dancing around in a boxer's jig.

I never wanted to say the awful things my mother said to me, but all the vows and good intentions in the world are powerless in the face of the modeling principle. Even though I am now able to control my hands when it comes to hurting, I still have trouble with my mouth. I have set some limits for myself to prevent name-calling and criticizing truly vulnerable areas. But when I get mad, I lose a lot of sensitivity. I'm afraid that when I'm mad enough, my goal is to hurt and I still find ways to do that. I'd like to think I've never done any permanent damage, but that's pretty naive.

The worst part of emotional hurting is that I'm not always aware of when I've stepped over my final limit line. I don't have the same safety switch for emotional abuse that I've developed for my children's physical protection. Sometimes I find out later that I've caused real pain. I feel bad when I discover that fact, but the damage has been done.

> *Don't let kids push your buttons.*

Don't let kids push your buttons. That aspect of good discipline is very important. Of course, that's the expert talking. She doesn't have any buttons. Poor Dragon Mom, on the other hand, has row upon row of buttons hiding right under her monster skin. They're mostly hidden, but the same little kids that learned by nine months of age to turn on the TV can quickly find each and every one of a dragon's buttons and become adept at pushing them. The motivation is exactly the same. Children love to feel the power of manipulating their environment—in this case, me.

The problem with a small brain is that once a button is pushed, an electrical pattern is activated. When we touch a hot surface, we automatically pull away. That part of our body is connected to a part of our brain that guarantees a certain response. We each have a "Hot surface!" button, which serves us well. But Dragon Mom has a number of buttons that don't serve her well. For example, when she issues a direct order and a child turns her back and does the opposite, a "Get furious!" button is activated, which doesn't serve anything, since no one is afraid of the dragon's anger. Here's an example:

✳✳✳✳✳✳✳✳✳✳

Child is scraping fingernails across a chalkboard.

Dragon says, "Stop that right this minute!"

Child smiles at Dragon Mom. Turning back to chalkboard, child produces another long, agonizing sound.

Dragon Mom explodes, jumps around yelling and screaming, makes a number of remarks about child's character and lack of sensitivity to the feelings of others, grabs child and takes chalkboard away. Sends child to room, where child gets out felt pens and starts drawing on wall.

✳✳✳✳✳✳✳✳✳✳

I know for a fact that my children have been known to push my buttons just to liven up an otherwise dull day. One of them admitted it once!

There is more to the human brain than reflexes, but poor Dragon Mom doesn't have a fully-developed human brain. She can't make decisions, but relies on automatic responses most of the time. However, she can learn simple things. I'm trying to teach her that when a button is pushed, she can pause for a minute instead of reacting instantly. That pause may enable her to make a decision. During a pause, she can decide not to issue a direct order unless she has the means and willingness to follow through without putting on a show for her kids' entertainment. Here is the same scene as the dragon would have played it if she hadn't continued reacting.

Child makes screeching sound.

Dragon Mom says, "That sound really bothers me. I wish you wouldn't do it."

That could be the end of the dialogue—if the child cared that the mother was bothered. If the child's intention was to bother, Mom could end the scene by leaving the room. Such matter-of-fact action takes the reward out of the behavior and makes it less likely to continue.

Here's a good rule to remember: *If children are doing inappropriate things for attention, the way to stop them is to take away the attention.* Not that they'll necessarily give up easily, but if you persist they will eventually stop. That's a scientific law, not just a made-up rule. Unfortunately, Dragon Mom has limited memory banks, so when she forgets, I have to forgive her. She isn't at all scientific in her approach to parenting!

Speaking of giving children attention, that's another important approach to discipline. Children who have their needs met—all of them, including the need for attention—are much less likely to demand heavy-handed discipline than those who are suffering need deficits. The principle operates on a simplistic as well as a more complex level.

For example, a hungry, tired child is more likely to misbehave than a rested, well-fed one. What a tired, hungry child needs first and foremost is not discipline, but food and rest. Discipline becomes unnecessary when needs are appropriately satisfied. On a more complex level, the child who feels neglected and unloved is more likely to cause problems than one who feels secure and cared for.

Of course, this is the expert speaking. Dragon Mom, faced with a hungry, tired, misbehaving child, is more likely to rave and threaten than to take care of the need. This response is partly because her own needs are not always met. She may be fed and clothed, but she seldom feels loved. I hope by giving her the attention she needs and trying hard to love her in this book, she'll quit misbehaving so much!

72

There's a Gap Between Stimulus and Response: Use It!

I was brushing my teeth one morning when my daughter slouched into the bathroom, wrapping her bathrobe around her. Instead of "Good morning," she angrily spat out, "Well? What do you want for your birthday?"

I was stunned at the disparity between the tone and content of the question. Shocked out of my usual pattern of an angry response, I just stared at her. My daughter didn't seem to need a response. She grunted, then turned and walked out, leaving only the sound of slippers shuffling down the hall.

Soon she was back, the anger gone from her face. We looked at each other, then broke into laughter.

"Why in the world were you so mad at me?" I asked her when we stopped to breathe.

"I wasn't mad at you," she admitted. "I'm just tired."

What I know:	I know how to feed my family nutritiously and make a mealtime pleasant. I know how to recognize game-playing and bids for attention.
What I do:	I fall right into my children's games.
Why:	When I'm Dragon Mom, my beady little eyes don't see very well. Besides, when I'm hungry I'm not very smart.

CHAPTER EIGHT
MEALS

I always had a vision of the way families should eat together–sharing conversation, enjoying each other's company. I'm not sure where I got this image. Perhaps I picked it up from books or movies; maybe it was my own invention. Wherever it came from, it was one of the motivating factors in wanting a large family. I dreamed of the wonderful mealtimes we would someday share.

In my own childhood, my family always sat down to dinner together. My memory is of a pleasant kind of ritual starting with grace and ending with being excused. There didn't seem to be a rule concerning what was talked about–somehow it just turned out to be mainly pleasant. Or perhaps the years have given a glow to my childhood mealtime memories.

Anyway, I started my family with this image in mind, and I could hardly wait for my first baby to be big enough to sit up at the table so that we could have a real family meal. If you have ever experienced a baby at the dinner table, you know that meals are hectic. It's fine if all you have to do is concentrate on the baby, but if you're trying to cook, serve, feed and entertain the baby as well as eat, you can just forget any kind of intelligent conversation.

But I didn't give up. I figured that eventually the baby would grow old enough to fit my image, so I kept the high chair at the table and endured. Of course, in a moderately large family like mine, the baby that grows up is replaced by the next baby. It was a number of years before there wasn't a baby in the high chair. In the meantime, each baby grew into an unruly toddler who not only demanded individual attention at mealtime, but had ways to get it!

One of the circumstances in my family is that for a good number of my parenting years the children outnumbered the adults at the dinner table. That was never true when I was a child. I grew up in my grandparents' house, because my mother was a single parent. There were three, sometimes four adults to two children. Looking back now, I can see that the child-adult ratio makes a big difference in what happens at meals.

My childhood dinnertime memory starts after I was six and my sister four. There were no toddlers at these wonderful meals, which may explain why I have pleasant memories.

When I became a parent many issues reared their ugly heads at mealtime, or lurked deep beneath both behavior and conversation. There were issues around messes, behavior expectations, what and how much to eat, and many more. These issues didn't start right away.

When my children were babies, there were no issues because I didn't expect anything from them. I knew there would be a mess. Table manners were a thing of the future, after they had learned to feed themselves with some skill. What to eat and how much wasn't an issue either, since I only presented a choice of nutritious foods. I firmly believed that it's bad to urge babies to eat. When they indicated they'd had enough, I quit feeding them. That was easy. If they skipped the peas one meal, I'd give them another vegetable at another meal. I believed that they would balance their own diets, and they did.

Mostly my children ate plenty as beginners, and feeding was a satisfying experience. I didn't have to deal with eating problems in my babies. My job was to offer and feed them what they indicated they wanted. It worked fine. I gave them the responsibility for what and how much to eat.

As they grew older, this method didn't work so well. I was no longer able to control the food they were offered. Once they got into the outside world, started going to birthday parties and watching television, my job got harder. At a progressively earlier age, each of my children discovered that there were a lot of more interesting things to eat than the plain, naturally wholesome foods I was giving them. Once that happened, I had a fight on my hands. My children still have vague resentments about the Easter baskets filled with trail mix. Nuts and dried fruit weren't exactly what they felt they deserved for a treat.

Portrait of the Perfect Lunch

I carefully selected a beautiful pear, ripe to perfection and without a blemish. Handling it like a newborn baby, I laid it gently in my son's lunch bag. I felt a moment of satisfaction.

When he came home from school, I asked, "How was the pear?" Then I held my breath, knowing I'd set myself up. I've seen the school trash after lunchtime. It's full of perfect fruit of all varietes—fruit packed by loving parents and discarded by uncaring children. I've watched those children gulp down the least nutritious parts of their lunches and rush off to play ball. It's a matter of priorities.

I was crestfallen. "You didn't throw it away?"

"No," he answered carelessly.

"Well, thank goodness!"

"I traded it for a candy bar."

Oh.

Maybe I was a fanatic. My children certainly thought so. I thought I was just doing my job. A scene about this issue sticks in my mind:

✳✳✳✳✳✳✳✳✳✳

"Mom, I'm hungry."

"But we just finished lunch!"

"I know. But I'm hungry."

"Well, have a snack. Here, take some fruit."

"Nah, I don't feel like fruit."

"Well, there are some carrots in the refrigerator."

"Yuck!"

"How about cheese and crackers? I'll fix them for you."

"I don't feel like cheese, and I hate those whole wheat crackers."

"A bowl of cereal?"

"Sure! You got Lucky Charms?"

"You know I never buy sugary cereal. It's bad for you—ruins your teeth."

"There's never anything to eat in this house. Other kids' moms have sodas, candy, and good stuff for snacks. I don't see why you treat us so awful!"

"Oh, stop it!" Dragon Mom is starting to puff up. "I'm sick of listening to you complain. If you want something to eat, get it yourself and leave me alone before I get really mad!"

"Go ahead and get mad. There's a law against child abuse, you know. And you're abusing me by not having snacks in the house. And the stuff you serve us for meals is yuck, too!"

I leave the room, pointy teeth gnashing, steam coming from my nostrils. My nine-year-old ignores me. He's pawing through the phone book, presumably looking up the telephone number to report me. You can see the attitude problem here.

✳✳✳✳✳✳✳✳✳✳

78

Feeling the way they did about what I chose to serve them, the next problem was predictable: how much they had to eat. I'm talking now about the clean plate syndrome.

I was never told to clean my plate as a child, but clean plates were modeled by every family member. What I didn't eat, my mother finished. I knew why: wasting food was wrong. She never preached it, but I was well aware of her value. She had been through a rough period with my father when there wasn't enough money for food, and this may have influenced her attitude. At any rate, she didn't make an issue of it, just quietly demonstrated her value over and over again.

When I sat at the table with my own children, I brought with me two conflicting values:

1. Children should be allowed to eat as little as they choose.
2. Food should not be wasted.

The solution to this dilema, of course, is to let children serve themselves and then insist that they eat all they have taken. When this method is used, children have choices and food isn't wasted. I know this intellectually, but somehow I never managed it. I just didn't trust them after they got old enough to make choices, because that's when the game-playing started. Not all of them played to the same extent, and the games make sense in light of the emotional tone at the table. Nevertheless, it was a big problem for me.

The snack scene is an example of the pattern. Complain about being hungry before the meal is ready. Help yourself to a snack if you can get away with it and if you can stand the yucky snack food that is available. If you can't get away with it, come to the table angry. Sit down at the meal and start the complaints.

Children often use mealtimes to express their need for power.

∗∗∗∗∗∗∗∗∗∗

"I'm not hungry, Mommy. Do I have to eat?"

"Well, maybe you're not hungry because you ate that box of crackers right before dinner."

"No, that's not the problem. I'm just not hungry. Can I get down and play?"

"No, and quit complaining!"

Then the next child would start (the one who hadn't gotten to the box of crackers before it was gone and so was mad at his brother, me, and everybody). Instead of expressing his anger, he started in on the food.

"I don't like broccoli! It smells bad."

"Well, eat your meat and rice."

"The meat isn't done enough and the rice makes me choke."

These two would fuss throughout the meal, begging all the while to get down and play. Sometimes the others would join them. Eventually, the meal would be over and they'd all leave the table, grateful that it was time to play at last.

Half an hour later: "Mom, I'm hungry. Can I have a peanut butter sandwich?"

"No!" I shout. "Next time, eat your dinner!"

I walk into the kitchen to discover another child eating a bowl of cereal. He has helped himself, leaving milk spilled on the counter, sugar on the floor.

Dragon Mom wakes up and explodes: "What's this horrible mess? We just finished dinner! If you wanted to eat, you should have eaten then. I won't have you making messes and eating all day long. I can't stand it! I just can't stand it!"

Swinging her tail across the floor, she grabs the cereal box, crushing it in her claws and sending tiny unsweetened "o's" of nutrition across the counter. "If I ever catch you eating again right after refusing your dinner, I'm going to make you sorry you were ever born!" She screams, shooting flames, "You kids are spoiled rotten! You just seem to want to ruin my life!"

The children quietly watch the terrible show of power. She's so angry that when she runs out of words, she picks up the half-filled bowl of cereal and milk and turns it over on the culprit son's head. Suddenly the room is quiet except for the sobs of the child with milk and tears streaming down his forlorn face.

Exit Dragon Mom. Enter Bodunky, who immediately puts on her apron, takes crying child in her arms, clucking comforting words to the others who have been watching the dragon's terrible show of power. Their expressions are calm; it's as if they seem to know they can just wait out this terrible monster attack.

Bodunky sweeps up the scattered cereal, wipes up the spilled milk, then puts the empty cereal bowl in the dishwasher. The comforted child leaves with the others, his hunger and his need for power both satisfied.

Before long, another child enters the kitchen where Bodunky is just finishing the cleanup.

"I'm hungry. Can I have a peanut butter sandwich?"

Without a word, Bodunky washes her hands, puts on a clean apron, and fixes a sandwich. It's now an hour after the meal. The dragon has gone back to sleep, and Mrs. Bodunky is not shocked by the request. End of game.

✳✳✳✳✳✳✳✳✳✳

Sometimes Dragon Mom didn't end the scene this quickly, but kept on so long that the problem didn't come to a head until almost time for the next meal. Then Bodunky's appearance and feeding behavior would ensure another round.

Writing about this now amazes me. It's so hard to see the game

81

while you're playing it, but so easy to see it from a distance. I can't believe I played this game for years and never did anything about it. But Dragon Mom just acts automatically. She doesn't have great insights, and she doesn't think much. She just feels mad, then guilty. The guilt brings on the appearance of Mrs. Bodunky, who is anxious to make up to everyone for the anger.

There are alternative approaches, of course, but Dragon Mom's beady little eyes and small mind can't ever see them. She doesn't understand game playing. She doesn't know about power struggles, except from a primitive point of view. If she had understood children's need to feel powerful and their ability to pick effective battlegrounds–like meal times–she would have found ways to grant power that didn't involve food. The expert knows this, but she just thinks. She doesn't parent. Janet C. Parent could have figured this out, too, even if the expert hadn't told her, but she was seldom invited to mealtimes.

If I had invited her, she could have taught Dragon Mom how to break the pattern by being less angry and more firm. Or she could have taken over and discarded the power stance altogether. She would have adopted the problem-solving mode that is her strength.

> *A problem-solving approach can reveal many causative factors.*

1. Janet C. would have examined the emotional tone of the meal to see whether that was the reason the children preferred to eat at other times.

2. She would have considered the attention factor: was each child getting enough attention at meals?

3. She would have thought about expectations for table behavior. If they were too high for the age of the child, she would have relaxed the standards a bit.

4. She would have worked hard to keep stress away from family meals.

5. In addition, Janet Competent Parent would have worked to increase appetites by ensuring that each child had plenty of air and exercise. She knows that appetite is the best motivation for eating, and that hungry children don't have as much need to play games as those whose appetites lag.

6. She would also have limited television or eliminated it altogether, since the tube and its commercials effectively dull normal, natural appetites through lack of exercise. It then replaces the natural ones with strong, persistent, nagging appetites for the products it so effectively sells. Even adults can't protect themselves from this replacement process, and little children are even more vulnerable.

If this is difficult to believe, stand in the cereal aisle of any supermarket for ten minutes and observe children and parents passing through. Notice how often children beg for the cereals that are made up of unsweetened natural ingredients. Compare this to the constant whining for those cereals filled with sugar, artificial colors and flavors that are heavily advertised on television.

Janet C. knows that none of her approaches to improving mealtime conditions is foolproof. She understands that feeding is an extremely complex issue. One of the difficulties is the fact that successful feeding and satisfactory weight gains are taken as signs of good parenting. This process starts in the first week of the child's life. If the newborn can't eat, or eats without weight gains, the parent in charge of feeding is going to feel enormous blame. If you start with that kind of pressure in week one, you aren't going to lose it in week two, or year two. Given that heavy responsibility weighing on the parent, and the power of the child to resist eating, meals can become emotional times.

> *Individual food needs will vary with different schedules and body rhythms.*

Add the fact that children have individual eating patterns, tastes, habits, and body schedules, even though you're trying to eat as a group. The problem is complex. The goal for me was family meals: all of us sitting together at the same time and eating basically the same food. With all those mouths to feed, I certainly wasn't about to take individual orders!

Here is an example of how individual body rhythms conflict with scheduled family mealtimes. One of my sons had great difficulty eating first thing in the morning. Unfortunately, I have always believed that children must start the day with a good breakfast. Sending a child to school with an empty stomach is a cardinal sin to me. Since breakfast was a required family meal, this child was served a hearty, hot breakfast, just like the others. Anxious to please, he forced it down on a daily basis.

I didn't realize that this created a problem until the time came when I had to give up family breakfast because everyone's schedule varied so greatly. At that time I discovered that this son did much better responding to his own body rhythm than he did forcing food into his stomach because of my ideas. It was an important lesson for me.

I still haven't figured out how to resolve the problem of family meals versus individual schedules and rhythms, but I've become a lot more relaxed about both. Actually, as I've grown older, I've become a lot more relaxed about everything!

Illness created other problems. Two of my children were frequently sick for their first six years, and the others had the usual run of childhood illnesses. Whenever a child would get sick, I would naturally respond to the change in appetite, diet, and schedule. I was very willing to pamper a sick child—one time when Mrs. Bodunky is an effective parent. However, my children quickly adjusted to ordering up special foods, which they were served in bed on their own schedules. The day after the illness was over, the scene was something like this:

✳✳✳✳✳✳✳✳✳✳

"Dinner time!"

"I don't feel like eating."

"That's okay. Just come to the table. I know you've been sick. You don't have to eat if you don't feel like it."

"Mommy, I feel like some 7-Up."

"Honey, you know we don't drink 7-Up for dinner. How about a glass of milk?"

"Nah." (The words, "No, thank you," never came easily to my children's lips.)

"Want some mashed potatoes?"

"Nah. But I'll take a peanut butter sandwich."

"Aha! So you are hungry."

"Yeah, a little. But I don't want any of that stuff."

✳✳✳✳✳✳✳✳✳✳

Mealtime issues are too complex for easy solutions.

I have finally come to see that I'll never solve all of the mealtime problems. But Janet Competent Parent's insights do better than Dragon Mom's stomping and threatening.

Still, it doesn't help to berate Dragon Mom. She doesn't learn to do better by being criticized. She has a better chance to improve if she feels loved and cared about. I think I'll turn off the computer now and go fix her favorite food. She loves chocolate cake. I'm even going to let her lick off the frosting!

What I know:	There are ways to put babies and small children to bed and keep them there with firm but gentle persistence.
What I do:	I lose patience if they cry or resist.
Why:	I don't have infinite patience. I let Dragon Mom put my children to bed.

CHAPTER NINE
BEDTIME

For many of the parents in the parenting classes and workshops I teach, the very word "bedtime" triggers anxiety. I've been surprised at the number of parents having so much difficulty putting their children to bed. I had my share of problems, but not like the parents I encounter now.

I've observed two patterns. In number one, the parent has no set bedtime, but believes children will go to bed when they are tired. He or she may lack company in the evening, so if the child's natural rhythm means staying up late, the parent doesn't mind. Having a child around during those lonely hours may fill a need.

Some children's natural body rhythms put them to sleep early in the evening, so there's no problem. There's also no problem if the child gets enough sleep by sleeping late in the morning or taking a long nap. Although this night-owl pattern for children is seldom approved by those who write parenting books, it works well for some families.

What doesn't work well is for the parent to use the child to meet his or her needs for company at the expense of the child's sleep. When this is happening, the child is always tired and hard to live with.

Another problem arises when the child resists sleep until he or she is overtired. These children often fuss a lot before collapsing in exhaustion. Such children ignore their own body signals and fight the very thing they need most–sleep. Without a firm adult to put these children in bed and insist that they stay there, they can have a miserable time. The "individual body rhythm" system doesn't always work. Some children need to be put to sleep before they become overtired. They can't do it on their own.

Another problem can occur in this night-owl pattern if the parent finds new company for the evenings. When the child is suddenly required to go to bed early, there will be a strong reaction. The child reacts to the change in philosophy–from natural body rhythm to an imposed, regular bedtime–and to the loss of an evening companion. Jealousy can rear its ugly head. Almost no child acquiesces quietly under these circumstances.

"Mommy, I don't want to go to bed. Let me stay up with you and Uncle Michael."

"Sweetheart, it's time for you to go to sleep."

"I'm not sleepy. Besides, I'm lonely in the bedroom all by myself."

"I'm sorry, darling, but you have to go to bed."

"Well, I won't! And you can't make me!"

Mommy and Uncle Michael are in for a long hard evening!

In the second pattern, the parent starts from the beginning to follow a pattern of regularly scheduled bedtimes. Not all children are ready for bed at the parent's designated bedtime. Those who take long naps in day care may come home ready for action rather than dinner and an early bedtime. These children will do fine with the parent who follows the body rhythm philosophy, but may resist the parent with the designated bedtime. Even a tired child who actually needs sleep at the scheduled time can give problems. That's when the power struggles come into play. Look at this scene:

✳✳✳✳✳✳✳

Parent has followed the established bedtime ritual exactly as it is carried out each night. Pajamas are on, teeth are brushed, story has been read, kisses given. Child is tucked into bed, favorite bear in arms, favorite pillow under head. The lights are low, soft music wafting. The setting is perfect for sleep. Parent tiptoes out, leaving child breathing evenly, eyes closed.

Parent picks up a good book and settles in. Three minutes of peace pass quickly by.

"Daddy!"

Parent gets up to see what child wants. What child wants is parent's company, but that's not what she says.

"I want a drink of water."

Parent gets drink, tucks child in again, leaves, settles down once again.

"Daddy..."

Repeat scene with different need. This can go on half the night, and often does. It is amazing how long parents will sometimes play this game before they blow up.

✳✳✳✳✳✳✳

> *Parents who don't have enough time to spend with their children may find it difficult to put them to bed.*

I once asked a group why they let this continue. After an extended discussion of how powerless they felt in this situation, it finally became clear that those with the greatest problem were those who regularly spent the day apart from their children. Thinking that the child might not have enough of their time and attention, they felt ambivalent about bedtime. Instead of gently but firmly insisting that the child go to sleep, they felt compelled to respond to each call. The cutoff point didn't

89

come until extreme emotion finally chased away the ambivalence and they refused to put up with the game any longer. This game was, in effect, the way these parents spent the evening with their children—even though it wasn't satisfying to either party.

I can't say that I'm perfect at getting children to sleep, but this is one area in which I have fewer ambiguous feelings than many other parents. Perhaps the way I have dealt with the ambiguity is to regularly change my philosophy. I've tried both patterns described above, and both worked for me.

> *A successful experience with one child can lead to false confidence.*

With my first baby, I started with firm ideas about sleep. Since he was a "good" baby, meaning that he didn't cry very much, I put him to sleep in his own crib in his own room, closed the door, and that was that. The pacifier the doctor recommended to "satisfy his sucking instinct" helped too. After the first few weeks, when he woke in the night I gave him the bottle of water recommended by the doctor. He soon figured out that it wasn't worth waking up for water, and he started sleeping through the night. If I had only had one baby, I would have thought I knew everything about putting babies to sleep!

Baby number two broadened my view and humbled me a bit. He was not an "easy" baby, which means he cried a lot more than the first one. The methods that had worked so well before didn't work at all with him. And by then, baby number one had grown up some, started having ear infections, and often woke up crying in the night. As a result, he spent a good deal of time sleeping with Mommy.

So, although I slept fairly well during my first year of parenthood, all of that changed drastically the second and third year. Life after dark got harder.

Then baby number three was adopted from Hong Kong and, like many children who come to adopted families from overseas, she regularly screamed at night. She didn't wake up, but her screams were enough to bring me running. When she finally slept peacefully all night, baby number four was born. I have to admit that I didn't sleep much for about seven years. But since I had chosen a big family, I just figured this was part of the picture. I'm a person that can make the most out of whatever sleep I get, so that helps too.

By baby number four, I had given up all firm ideas about putting children to sleep. My philosophy at that point was: whatever works! What worked was letting the youngest stay up until the big kids were ready for bed, then putting them all in bed at the same time. That way, he had company. He really resisted being taken away from the group and put away in a crib behind a closed door, my original method. Besides company, he had a bottle. Thanks to strong dental genes, he didn't get bottlemouth! If he woke in the night, I brought him into bed with me. I began to get more sleep, and I felt hardly any guilt about my lax approach.

Then, after a thirteen-year gap, I gave birth to my last baby. Since he was like another first child, I decided to go back to my original method so that I could have my evenings free. But I didn't figure his prematurity into this plan. He was a sick baby for three and a half months. When he finally came home from the hospital, he was still frail and fragile, and at high risk for SIDS—Sudden Infant Death Syndrome. I wasn't about to put him in a separate room behind closed doors. I didn't feel very good about letting him cry either, even though I knew he needed to go to sleep. So I did what seems very natural to many mothers, and indeed is the method of many cultures. I nursed him to sleep and then put him down. When he woke in the night, I took him in bed with me and nursed him some more. This approach prevents babies from learning how to put themselves back to sleep, which is a requirement for sleeping through

91

the night. He didn't learn independence in this area. He needed me for a long time. I didn't get a full night's unbroken sleep for several years! I'm not sorry, though. I was ready for a new method, even if it meant sacrificing my own sleep.

Now that I have watched myself go from one philosophy to another, I'm less inclined to tell people how to put babies to sleep. I am willing to help them sort out their options and the consequences of each.

I'm more certain about toddlers and preschoolers. I like my evenings to myself, so firm resolve is easy for me. I am free from ambivalence. I have to admit that Dragon Mom makes a regular appearance if there is a second request for a drink of water, but she isn't at her wildest. And she never gives in to Bodunky, which means I don't feel guilty about getting mad. When I have a good book or company to look forward to, it's an easy matter to be firm with a child who continues to call from the bedroom.

Of course, nothing is ever perfect, and even my firmness about bedtime for toddlers and preschoolers didn't work 100%. For years my daughter and I struggled with bedtime.

✻✻✻✻✻✻✻✻✻✻

"Five more minutes to play and then it's bedtime."

"Geeze, Mom..."

"Playtime is up. It's bedtime. Please get ready."

"Geeze, Mom. Just a few more minutes."

"No. I'll be back in five minutes to see if you're ready for bed."

Five minutes later. "Do you have your pajamas on and your teeth brushed? What? You're still playing? What did I tell you?"

"Uh. I don't know."

No child of mine can ever answer the question, "What did I tell you?"

"Put your pajamas on now!"

92

"Geeze, Mom!"

Not only did she drag her heels about moving toward the bed, but once there, she would lay awake–it seemed to me that she would actually force herself to stay awake–for long hours.

Eventually, I'd come in and yell at her.

"Go to sleep right now! Do you understand me?"

"Geeze, Mom!"

No child of mine has ever answered the question, "Do you understand me?" in the affirmative.

Even as a baby, she'd keep herself awake. I'd come in and find her standing in her crib an hour after she'd been put there. It wasn't until I laid her down and stood over her that she would finally go to sleep.

I was very determined, and I always won, but she put up a good fight, night after night, year after year. The struggle continued into the late elementary school years. Unlike my other children, she never seemed to take responsibility for going to bed at a reasonable hour on her own. She wouldn't go to bed until I insisted. One summer, I got tired of the fight.

"Stay up as late as you want." I told her.

"OK!" was her response.

And she did! For several months, she stayed up all night. She kept herself well occupied, sewing and baking brownies in the wee hours of the morning. Around 5:00 a.m., she'd start getting ready for bed. I wouldn't see her again until late afternoon. This schedule kept up until school was ready to start again. Then suddenly, with no explanation, she switched her schedule and put herself to bed at 9:00 from then on. In fact, she became fanatic about it, and suffered a great deal if something kept her up later. I never again told her when to go to bed.

This method was called "the ecstasy of excess" by one of my early childhood teachers, Betty Jones. It is based on the idea that when people get to do something they need to do in a thorough way, they get it out of their system and the need disappears. I believe in this principle and try to remember to use it when there has been a long hard struggle over something.

Naptime is a different story. I'm much more lax about naps. My reasons stem from several sources: my own history, my leaning toward the "natural body rhythm" philosophy, and my own selfishness about being tied to home by a scheduled nap time.

As a child, I hated naps. My mother let me give them up by the age of two. During periods of my life when I was forced to lie down, I hated every minute. The "resting" part of kindergarten and naps at summer camp live in my memory as sheer agony. Even today, I dislike interrupting my waking hours with daytime sleep. When I wake up, I want to start a new day, not continue with the old one.

I know that a two-year-old who objects to naps will relearn to settle down and go to sleep after an initial period of resistance, but at the first sign of resistance to naps from one of my children, I gave in. This often resulted in strange behavior at dinner time.

✳✳✳✳✳✳✳✳✳✳

"What's wrong with Bret? His eyes are half shut!"

"I guess he's sleepy because he didn't want to take a nap today."

"Bret, eat your dinner, and then you can go to bed."

"Bret! Bret!"

Too late. Poor Bret had laid his head right on top of the lamb chop and was fast asleep.

✳✳✳✳✳✳✳✳✳✳

But the sleepy dinnertime stage always passed rapidly and we both enjoyed the feeling of freedom that resulted when we weren't tied to a regular afternoon nap schedule.

This leniency about naps did hamper my ability to use most day care programs. Most preschool age programs have a very firm napping policy. Like many parents, day care workers use naptime to renew themselves or to catch up on things they can't do while children are awake. They can't have children demanding their attention during this period. They use the firm resolve method at naptime, insisting that all children lie down and at least be quiet. I wasn't willing to subject my non-napping children to that routine, so at times I had to get quite creative in figuring out day care arrangements.

Since I've made so many changes in philosophy about putting children to sleep, it might seem that I act on whims. Actually, behind my philosophies is a definite goal—independence for my children. It's just that I've changed my mind about how to reach it. Originally, my idea of independence was based on the rugged individualism this country is famous for. My approach was to start early. That's why I taught my first children to put themselves to sleep from day one in a room separate from mine.

> *Meeting a child's needs is the first step in fostering independence.*

What I didn't understand then is that the way to independence is to first thoroughly fulfill a child's dependent needs. Pushing for independence too early can cause them to be even more dependent.

Waiting too long can be just as big a problem. The trick is to decide just when you're filling actual needs and when you've crossed the line, keeping your child dependent on you for your own purposes rather than for their good.

> *Other cultures have different parenting goals.*

I see this line differently from the way I used to because of my experience with families from cultures other than my own. In some cultures, the goal is not that the children grow up and leave the parents, but that they stay closely connected with the parents and eventually assume an adult role. The goal is not separation, but attachment, not independence, but interdependence. In these cultures, the line between keeping the child dependent for your own purposes rather than for their good is the opposite end of the scale from where I used to draw the line.

All of this was very confusing to me as I began to notice that these children who seemed to be dependent for what I considered to be too long grew up to live normal, functional lives. They also remained closer to their families than many of the more "independent" children I had been used to, an outcome that appeals to me now that I'm getting older.

Parents in these cultures tend to sleep with their children from birth, never putting them in separate cribs or behind closed doors. If they haven't switched to bottle feeding, swayed by the purposeful marketing of formula companies, they nurse frequently, rather than putting the child on a schedule or trying to get the child to sleep through the night. I'm not saying these methods are right or wrong. It is just a different way to achieve the goal of helping the child to become a functional adult.

Sleeping is just one area in which my point of view has changed over the period of my parenting career. Toilet training is another. The next chapter deals with that subject.

What I know:	When children are ready, toilet training isn't hard.
What I did:	I got impatient before they got ready.
Why:	I followed good advice the first time and had success. I gave myself full credit for the success. With my puffed-up sense of power, I went about training the second child much earlier and met with frustration.

CHAPTER TEN
TOILET TRAINING

In my memory, toilet training was mostly no big deal. That's because I remember the good times and the easy children. I really wanted to write about them, but Dragon Mom wants to tell her experience.

I had great patience with the first child. I waited until he was well over two, then made only gentle suggestions. When he seemed to have some control over the matter, I offered rewards. Everything worked! I couldn't figure out why toilet training was such a problem for so many people.

When the second child came along, I was still riding the crest of my first success. (Notice that I credited myself with the success—not the first child.) The summer before my second son was two, I decided that since I was so good at toilet training, I might as well give it a shot.

✳✳✳✳✳✳✳✳✳✳

One sunny morning, I announced at breakfast that there would be no more diapers. Oh, mistake!

I dressed my second son in "big boy pants" and sent him and his brother out to play in the yard. "Tell Mommy when you have to go pee pee," I said cheerfully. Five minutes later, he was at the back door, silently pointing to the growing spot on his pants and the wet streaks on his legs.

"Here's the potty," I announced, too late.

"Well," I thought to myself, "he's aware of what's happening. That's a good start." My theory was that diapers created a lack of awareness, and the first step was to make him conscious of urinating.

Well, the awareness soon faded. He quickly adjusted to using his little shorts just like his bulky diapers; they just didn't hold as much. After the first time, he didn't bother to show me. By 10:00 a.m. the potty was still dry and the pile of wet big-boy pants was still growing. Reaching in the drawer for a clean pair and discovering none, I made a mental note to load the washing machine. Then, tugging on his bathing suit, I suggested, "Let's turn on the sprinklers."

The sprinklers took care of the problem for the rest of the morning. Running around in a wet bathing suit wasn't so awful. Who knew where the moisture came from anyway? He seemed happy that I had quit bugging him about the potty. At lunch time, I sent him through the sprinklers once more, then put diapers on him for lunch and nap time.

After the nap, I took off the wet diapers, showed him the potty after it was too late, redressed him in shorts still warm from the dryer, and sent him outside again. By evening, my patience had begun to fade—but not my determination.

Changing his shorts for the hundredth time, I gritted my teeth. I silently vowed not to get angry. And I didn't until I caught him on the living room rug with the dog, totally oblivious to the stream running down both legs into a puddle at his feet.

"What are you doing?" I screamed in my dragon voice. I went into the full act, jumping around, swinging my huge scaly tail, and threatening

98

this innocent child with my sharp teeth and long claws.

He didn't seem to understand what the ruckus was about. He reached down, pulled off his wet pants, left them in the puddle on the rug, and ran out of the room behind the dog. I don't remember what I did, but I probably followed my pattern and called out Bodunky to clean up the mess and comfort the child. End of day one.

❋❋❋❋❋❋❋❋❋❋

I don't know why I didn't see the light at that point. This child was not ready to be toilet trained. He had never given any signals of readiness. The reasonable thing was to back off and wait–especially if I was going to get so upset.

But parents aren't always reasonable. Somewhere in the back of my head was a piece of advice from a well-meaning but unknowledgeable person: "Once you start toilet training, never give up!" Well, I took that advice.

It was a long, hard summer. And fall. And winter. I washed about a million pairs of pants. I wore out my washing machine, my dryer, and even a clothesline or two. It's hard to believe I could have been so blind and stubborn toilet training this poor son. Looking back, I can see that when I waited until my children were ready, willing, and able to be trained, it was easy.

> *For toilet training to be successful, a child needs to demonstrate three kinds of readiness .*

Toilet training is not difficult if you can keep relaxed about what age it begins. There are three signs of readiness. Children need to *understand* what is expected, they need to *be able to* comply, and they need to *be willing to* comply. That is, they need to be intellectually, physically, and emotionally ready.

Physical readiness is a matter of control–they have to be able to hold on and let go at the proper time in the proper place. Timing is crucial, and has a lot to do with the child's muscle power. In addition, the child needs to be able to handle his or her own clothing, another physical skill.

Intellectual readiness is on its way when the child becomes aware of his or her body processes. A beginner toilet trainee often points out wet or poopy diapers after the fact. That's a start.

Lack of emotional readiness can create enormous problems. If the child is stubborn, defiant, or rebellious, you're bound to have a power struggle on your hands if you insist on use of the potty. Somehow, you need to convey the message that you are a supporter of independence, not a threat to it. If you impose your will, the child's toilet training won't be easy.

Some children are anxious to please. Willingness is no problem. Rewards may work for those who are not so anxious to please. The best motivation, however, comes from the inner rewards children receive from growing in skills and responsibility.

It helps parents relax if they know the real statistics instead of listening to stories of wonder children who were fully trained at fifteen months. The facts indicate that the average age when children can use the potty or toilet by themselves with minimum accidents is around two and a half. Night time dryness comes even later.

> *There are different objectives in toilet training.*

By my definition, the task of toilet training is not accomplished if the parent is still in charge or needed. That's because my immediate goal is the child's independence. I realize that some parents have a different goal: they want to get rid of diapers as soon as possible. With that goal, you don't just sit around and wait for a couple of years. You start as soon as you think you can get some results, which with some children is within the first year.

My mother, who washed diapers by hand, took this second approach. She claimed that I was trained by a year old. I used to scoff at that claim without recognizing that both her goal and her definition of "trained" were different from mine. We didn't discuss these differences much. I scoffed and she criticized, saying I was "lazy" about toilet training my children.

As I became acquainted with families from different cultures I was able to see this "catch 'em early" approach from a more accepting point of view. I still wouldn't want to try it myself. It takes a lot of energy and attention to predict exactly when something's going to come out of a baby! If you do use this approach, my advice is to be careful not to get angry or pressure the child. Harsh toilet training can leave serious aftereffects. Also, this approach works better if you're with your baby every minute. You can't just put them out in the yard to play, as I did. If you have a life outside parenthood or work outside the home, forget it!

When you're in the process of toilet training, it seems as though it will never end. Perspective helps all that. Many years after toilet training my last child, I can see that it wasn't as long or as bad as it seemed at the time. If you're having trouble, I hope you will read on and discover where your difficulties lie so you won't feel like putting on dragon rages as I did with my second son.

> *Power struggles can delay toilet training.*

One source of difficulty is the power struggle that sometimes develops over toilet training. If you and your child are butting heads, you're doomed to suffer. There's just no way you can control the child's elimination once he or she decides to defy you. If you think about it, you don't want to control these processes anyway; you want the child to assume responsibility. Often these power struggles get going because the parent started the training process before the child had reached full readiness. Then rather than giving in and accepting defeat, the parent stubbornly persists, as I did. If you are in a power struggle, let go. Stop pushing.

Another possible cause of problems is if you jump the gun when the first sign of readiness appears. If the child is physically ready but doesn't understand what's expected, modeling can help. That's one advantage of putting a child in day care. There are lots of child models.

Sometimes the child only <u>seems</u> to be physically ready. He or she can hang on, but can't let go at will. Deliberately relaxing muscles takes a different kind of control. If a child doesn't have it, you can't force it. It's a matter of time and skills that just can't be taught. It's frustrating to offer a potty without results to a child who's been dry for several hours and whose bladder must be full. You know that as soon as the pants are back on—boom!

> *Attitudes toward diapering can effect toilet training.*

Sometimes difficulties arise because of a long history of struggles over diapering. (Although this ongoing struggle can make training attractive to the child who perceives that at long last she will be in charge and won't have to suffer the diapering process!)

Your attitude toward diapering can make the difference between constant struggle and teamwork. The child will go through at least a few uncooperative periods; it's part of growing up. The first phase commonly begins when the baby first learns to roll over. It's difficult to diaper a squirming, rolling baby. If you continue to try for cooperation and involve the baby in the process, eventually this phase will pass and peace will reign until the next phase.

102

This time comes when the baby resents being interrupted at work or play and refuses to lie down. Don't give up on the concept of teamwork when this happens. Keep trying to involve the child, rather than strong-arming. Your work will pay off in another period of peace. If diapering is more of a shared experience and less of a power play on your part, toilet training becomes a more natural step.

I realize that all of this sounds easier than it is when you're in the process. And sharing an experience that may be sticky or unpleasantly smelly is nobody's idea of fun. But if you react to the smells and stickies rather than to the baby, you give a strong message about the body and its products that may set attitudes that interfere with toilet training.

If you can be matter-of-fact or even–God help you!–appreciative, you'll find that the child will also be matter-of-fact about body products. You may even find the child proudly displaying one of these precious products that he has finally managed to deposit in a potty instead of in his diaper. That is the day you know you've succeeded. All the diapering efforts have paid off.

How can you get out of power struggles once they've begun? One way is to let go. If you've been pushing your child to use the potty and you're meeting with resistance, just stop pushing. The results may surprise you.

Sometimes a well-trained child suddenly takes a giant step backward when a new baby comes into the family.

❋❋❋❋❋❋❋❋❋❋

"What? Wet pants again? That's your third accident this morning. What in the world is going on? You're a big boy now. You don't pee in your pants."

If child doesn't look properly ashamed, the dragon will enter, snorting fire.

"Just look at you! Now your good pants are all wet and you'll have to put on the ugly ones. Well, that's what you deserve!"

Child is now showing some discomfort, but once Dragon Mom's on-button is pushed, she can't stop. Somewhere deep inside herself, she knows that she should not shame this child. Rather than triggering her safety switch, this knowledge activates her augmentation button.

"Okay! You just go change those pants right this minute. No, I'm not going to help you. I don't care if you stand there dripping wet all day. I'm not going to do another thing for you!"

※※※※※※※※※※

> *The expert would never shame a child.*

At this point, the expert inside me is having a fit, shaking her fist at the dragon. She's knows how harmful it is to shame a child. Her words tumble out on top of each other. She explains the child's point of view—how it feels to be suddenly toppled from your position in the family by a new baby. This dethroning can be a very painful experience, creating feelings of loss, anger, fear, and jealousy. The stress and insecurity may cause the child to regress.

Furthermore, he may see from his dethroned position that this baby who is getting all the love and attention wears diapers in which he poops and pees. He may subconsciously think that if he poops and pees in his pants he can share in the limelight with the new baby. When parents respond with anger or punishment or both, stress on the child is even greater, which may cause further loss of control of the elimination process. If the parent responds with understanding and tries hard to give increased attention to the dethroned child, the chances are good that the child will decide it's okay to be older.

Does Dragon Mom listen to this lecture from the expert? Of course not. Her ears are as small as her brain and eyes. Her level of sensitivity is nil. She is still screaming criticism.

Has she ruined this child? Of course not. His psyche is probably bruised as a result of this scene. I feel sorry about that, and when the dragon returns to regular size, she will too. It's better if children grow up unbruised and unscarred, but asking parents never to get angry is asking the impossible.

What does Dragon Mom toilet training do to children? Can they survive intact? Sure. Children are good at surviving the effects of less-than-ideal training. But I don't recommend Dragon Mom's methods on a daily basis. It is better when competent parents, or at least Bodunkys, take the major role. The dragon blows up too often and goes too far in criticism. She can create problems that won't go away by themselves. It's unfortunate when that happens, because therapy is needed, although we seldom see that extreme result.

It doesn't take an expert to toilet train a child. It takes a little common sense, understanding, sensitivity, and patience. Dragon Mom is low on these qualities, but each of us has in us a competent parent and some sort of normal-sized Bodunky who can work together to counteract the dragon's storms.

> What I know: One should be open with children, encourage them to ask questions, and answer honestly and factually.
>
> What I did: I blew it!
>
> Why: Caught off-guard, I acted out my own education and upbringing.

CHAPTER ELEVEN
SEX EDUCATION

Because I thought toilet training was such a breeze, it would be logical to assume that I had an easy time with sex education. After all, the same or similar organs are involved. Actually, I started out all right, but I eventually messed up. In this case, I can't really blame the dragon's small brain. It was history that created the problems.

I had definite plans for the sex education of my children. I made those plans early in life, determined not to do to them what had been done to me. I wanted the openness about such matters that was lacking in my own childhood.

A brief look at my family history will explain. My grandmother, a product of the Victorian era, had never mentioned a word about sexual matters to my mother except to tell her, and later me, that God gave women babies. I don't think she was trying to convince us that babies come from virgin births; she just didn't want to go into details.

As a young person, I knew that babies and marriage usually went together. I wondered how God knew a woman was married. I never did figure it out, but I remember the day I found out that you didn't have to be married to have a baby.

✳✳✳✳✳✳✳✳✳✳

It was a clear, pre-smog, southern California day. I was in the back seat of my grandmother's car on the way to the beach, listening intently to the conversation up front between my mother and grandmother about an unmarried fifteen-year-old who had just given birth. The voices drifting back were expressing disapproval about this event.

"What's wrong with that?" I piped up, causing two heads to turn and look at me.

My grandmother mumbled something unintelligible and swerved away from the curb she was headed for. My mother sat silently, picking a loose thread on the towel she was holding.

"God doesn't make mistakes..." I continued, expounding a recent Sunday School lesson. The silence from the front seat was a strong message. I decided not to expound. I wrapped myself tighter in the towel covering my bathing suit and sat back. I considered this birth a miracle, but they obviously didn't. They were not about to tell me why.

This approach to sex education was not new in our family. I later heard the following from my mother.

✳✳✳✳✳✳✳✳✳✳

After twenty-one years of silence about sexual matters, my grandmother decided to educate my mother. She chose the night before my mother's wedding. With the announcement, "We need a little talk," she led her daughter out of the living room where the family was gathered around the fireplace. The two entered the master bedroom and settled themselves opposite each other on the twin beds my grandparents slept in. Taking my mother's hands in hers and looking her straight in the eye, my grandmother began, "I have something to tell you about...ummm...the facts of life."

My mother quickly tore her hands away, stood up, and said,

108

"Don't be ridiculous, Mother! I know all that!" She turned her back and strode proudly from the room.

❋❋❋❋❋❋❋❋❋❋

No one will ever know what my grandmother had in mind to tell her. She had waited far too long. And no one will ever know whether my mother really had it straight or not. She was as silent with me as my grandmother had been with her. And she skipped the prewedding talk.

What Do We Teach Girls about Being Female?

I remember my initiation into womanhood. First, there was THE MOVIE. We've all seen THE MOVIE. After the movie came the wait. Two years, to be exact, from fifth grade to seventh. I knew the secret, but hadn't yet joined the club.

Then came the Saturday with the backache and by Monday morning I was a woman. I was initiated in the girls' locker room of my junior high school. I announced quietly to my friend that I had "started" over the weekend. In a moment the news had flashed around the room and girls were coming up to congratulate me. Strange, even though most called it "the curse," there was still a distinction bestowed on those who experienced their first period. I was a celebrity for a day. I remember it well.

Parents today are beginning to regard menarchy as an important milestone deserving a rite of passage, instead of leaving it to the locker room gang. They feel it's important to teach that having a female body is not a curse, but a cause for celebration.

By the time I was ten I had rejected the theory that God puts babies in women's stomachs and had begun to wonder what the real story was. Growing up in a woman-dominated, single-parent extended family I also wondered periodically what God had put men on earth for. They seemed a bit superfluous to me. At the same time, I was experiencing what was then called "puppy love," body changes, sexual thoughts, and lots of questions. My mother avoided all my questions, apparently feeling she had done her duty by vaguely explaining menstruation, which became clear after I saw a movie at school.

During an overnight visit with a friend, the discussion in the wee hours of the morning turned to sex. Discovering my ignorance, my friend suggested that I needed to know the facts of life. She, however, refused to tell me. "Ask your mother," she advised.

I did. My mother said only, "I'll get you a book from the library."

She never did. End of sex education at home. The subject never came up again.

So when it was my turn to be a parent, I resolved to do a good job of educating my children. And I did, up until the day I blew it. I answered questions right and left. Where do babies come from? No problem. I had ready answers to every question my preschoolers came up with. I was confident and secure. I was open, honest, and developmentally appropriate.

Then came the fateful day. My children were six, four, three, and one when I ruined everything. I remember the scene well.

✳✳✳✳✳✳✳✳✳✳

The family was seated around the dinner table. Several conversations were in progress – none about sex education. The meal was progressing nicely for a change, which means everyone was eating, no one was throwing food on the floor, and the milk had not yet spilled.

My oldest son was eating silently, not part of any conversation. He was well educated about reproductive matters. He knew all about eggs and sperm, conception, gestation, and birth. He did not know about intercourse. Somewhere between a bite of mashed potatoes and a bite of peas, he noticed a gap in his knowledge.

He put down his fork and looked at me. "Mom?" His voice cut through someone else's sentence. I looked at him. On his face was the look he always got when processing information. Since sex education had not been a topic at that meal, I had no way of knowing what

110

information he was processing.

"Yes?" I responded innocently, little knowing what was to come.

With four little kids at a dinner table, there is seldom a moment of silence. But strangely enough, the babble died down at that very moment and all ears were listening as his question came out of the clear blue sky.

"How does the daddy's sperm *get to* the mommy's egg?"

The words hung in the air over the table. All eyes turned to me as each child waited for the answer. I searched my memory banks for a response that would be appropriate for all these little ears. I had been prepared to explain this part of the process. Of course I was. But not to the whole group. And not over dinner.

The pause lengthened. Never again would they all be so quiet for so long. My fork idled, shoving my peas into my mashed potatoes. I was frantically searching for the right words. I never found them. I heard my voice saying, "I'll tell you later." I might have even said, "I'll get you a book from the library."

✳✳✳✳✳✳✳✳✳✳

I did talk to him later. I'm sure I handled it calmly, though I don't recall much about that particular scene. But nothing I could say would change that first message of silence. I blew it. All of my children learned that this was no ordinary subject they could discuss anytime with Mom. This was a touchy one. As a result, the questions that had been so free and easy dried up and blew away. And as they got older, the children shied away whenever I brought up the subject.

Except for one son. This son's approach has really given me something to think about. He apparently decided to educate his mom and help her become open and relaxed, like she's supposed to be. He would tell me dirty jokes and ask me questions I didn't want to answer. Although I wanted to be available for discussions, I didn't want to deal with dirty jokes or discuss what I think is inappropriate between parents and children—like the details of my sex life. I didn't discuss what I consider my private life with my children, and—not surprisingly—they didn't want to discuss theirs with me.

I have felt uncomfortable about this conflict between being open and being private for a long time. Eventually, I came to understand that as children grow toward adulthood some kind of barriers need to be raised to protect children and parents from being stimulated by each other's sexuality. The statistics on the frequency of sexual abuse of children by parents show what can happen if appropriate barriers are not present.

I'm not saying that parents who are completely open about sexual matters end up abusing their children. I am only saying that reasonable barriers make sense to me now. Perhaps this is rationalization, but nevertheless I have quit apologizing to myself.

Sex education is not an area of parenting I brag about. I am seldom the parent I want to be. However, I am coming to love the parent I am. I hope that will happen to you, too!

What I know:	I have been trained to teach children, to facilitate their learning, and to learn from them.
What I do:	I get impatient, frustrated, and downright angry when teaching. Sometimes I get too busy with my own things to facilitate learning in my children. Often, I'm too involved in my own perspective to learn from my children.
Why:	Can't you guess by now? I'm a dragon.

CHAPTER TWELVE
TEACHING AND LEARNING

Early education is a subject near and dear to my heart, since that's the focus of my expert's expertise. She knows that children learn from day one, and so do parents. And they both teach. The roles are interchangeable. The teaching the child does is not so obvious, but it is important. Children must teach their parents who they are, what they are like as individuals. If parents are good observers and able to step out of their own skins and leave their own issues aside, they'll learn a great deal about their children. If they only look from their own perspective, or see only what they want to see, they'll miss a lot.

But, of course, that's the expert talking. The dragon, in spite of being so closely associated with an early childhood educator, has a different story. Here's an example of Dragon Mom teaching her child:

✳✳✳✳✳✳✳✳✳

I was ready to teach my first son to tie his shoelaces, and I think he was ready to learn. Perhaps he was not, because a problem soon developed. Anyway, he was interested in learning, and we sat together on the floor.

"Try it like this," I said, patiently showing him the first step.

He twisted and turned the laces together, not managing. "I can't," he said, his voice catching.

"Sure you can." I was still patient. I showed him once again.

"It's too hard." He pulled the shoe off and threw it on the floor.

"Come on! You can do it." My voice sounded strained now. I felt my teeth gritting. I brought the shoe back and put it on his foot. I took his little hands in mine, determined to help him.

He wrenched his hands free, took the shoe off again, and threw it at me. Then he burst into tears and ran for his bedroom, slamming the door. End of lesson one.

Lesson two was worse. By the time it ended, we were both in tears. I was brave until he shouted at me and blamed me for his failure.

"Forget the blankety-blank shoelaces!" I finally screamed, stalking from the room. Then I felt terrible! I had failed miserably, screaming at my innocent child, who was only trying to learn a self-help skill. What did I do?

I brought in Mrs. Bodunky, who went right out and bought him a pair of loafers. By the time he outgrew those, it was summer. She bought him a pair of sandals that buckled, so he managed just fine. This episode was before velcro, or he might never have learned to tie!

Finally the day came when he wanted a pair of tennis shoes for school, so I bought them for him. Mrs. Bodunky argued for another pair of loafers, but he couldn't run in them very well. Mrs. Bodunky tied the laces for him, carefully avoiding the trauma of further lessons. She used double knots so they wouldn't come untied at school.

Then one day I saw him sitting on the floor tying his shoes! I tried to be cool, since he hadn't mentioned this accomplishment to me and he obviously wasn't trying to draw attention to it now.

"Where did you learn to do that?" I gasped.

"Oh, Aunt Margaret taught me," he said, running out the door.

"Nothing to it," Aunt Margaret said later. "I just showed him how. It was easy." Did I notice a slight hint of accusation that he had to go to his aunt since his mother had failed to teach him? I was sensitive in those days about whether I was a good mother.

✻✻✻✻✻✻✻✻✻✻

I might have been expected to give up teaching my children then and there, but I didn't. I was, however, more aware of the inherent difficulties when I went into the teacher mode. As the children got older and were truly motivated to learn something from me, teaching got easier. I remember teaching this same son to change a tire, and we both felt proud of ourselves when the lesson was over.

THE TEACHABLE MOMENT

Here's a toddler imitating her mother as she cleans off the table. The child takes a plate when her mother's back is turned. Unfortunately, she drops it and it breaks. Her angry mother gives her a whack, then sends her away. The moment when the child was teachable is lost.

Instead of sorting out what went wrong, and learning how to carry plates so they don't drop, the little girl focuses on the smack and her feelings about it. Because she's now in the other room, she won't learn what to do if a plate breaks and needs to be swept up. She does learn that helping can get her into trouble, and that it's not okay to make a mistake.

Right after a mishap is when children are most open to learning. That's why it's so important not to scare them with heavy-handed discipline. We parents are teachers every moment of our waking lives. It's important that we give thought to *what we teach* and *how we are teaching it*.

Like many parents, I tried to teach my children to read. I tried it on my first son, the guinea pig, even before the shoelace lesson. I tried to

115

get him to say the names of plastic alphabet letters that I stuck on the refrigerator. He pulled them off and threw them on the floor. I spelled words with alphabet soup letters. He ate them. I tried to show him how to write his name. He scribbled. I gave up.

What I didn't understand then is that I should have approached reading as I did toilet training. Let me explain. Toilet training is easy when the child is ready. It can be very difficult when he is not. The same is true of learning to read. My child was not interested in the activities I presented, and he didn't like my pressuring him. Luckily, I went off to preschool and learned some facts that helped a lot. I backed off from pushing him. I quit worrying.

What I learned was that a few children—very few—start reading at four. I was one who did, so that experience gave me a false expectation for my own children. Incidentally, I am not necessarily a better reader today than someone who didn't learn to read until six or seven. And if you believe in IQ scores, you'll find that my IQ is no higher than the later reader, either. Luckily, I enjoy reading, which often isn't true of those who start young—especially those who were pushed to read.

By the age of five, a few more children are making sense out of printed words, but certainly not the bulk of them. In a group of five-year-olds, you'll find a number who are still as bored with print as my first son was. By six, many more children read, but not all. Some begin as old as seven, and others even at eight. What's hard to remember about this is that the four-year-old beginning reader isn't necessarily smarter than the eight-year-old beginning reader. But the messages each receives may influence self-esteem to a life-changing extent.

I was once involved with a private school for gifted and talented children. I discovered that only about half of the children in first grade were reading by the end of the year. In another year, most had become good readers. But they certainly didn't start out that way!

116

I don't mean to imply that with reading, as with toilet training, all you have to do is sit back and wait. You can promote reading in a number of ways. The most obvious ones are:

1. Read to them. Expose them to the world of stories and books.
2. Model. Read in front of them.
3. Model writing. Let them see you writing notes, letters, and lists. Make writing materials available, and you'll soon see them imitating you.
4. Turn off the TV and get them to play. Provide them with materials and encourage them in creative, imaginative play.

If you value play, you can go a long way in promoting it. And play is the most important way of all to get children ready to read. Through play, children gain feelings of power as they create and control their own worlds. These feelings are important in the acquisition of reading skills. They also increase muscular control. Coloring with crayons and felt pens on blank paper sharpens their eye-hand coordination, an important ability. Coloring books are not as good.

Like many parents, I believed in coloring books. I saw the benefits of learning to stay inside the lines. But I took a course in teaching children's art where the teacher explained how bad such pre-drawn pages were for children's developing creativity. He said children see adult drawings and are discouraged from producing their own because they don't measure up. "Don't draw for children," he advised, "and never, never give them coloring books or ditto sheets."

Well, I grabbed that idea, went home, and threw away all the coloring books and bought a ream of blank paper. Of course, as in everything I become fanatic about, it backfired.

My children who had experienced coloring books didn't really suffer at the loss, but one son was just a baby when I threw them all away, so he missed out completely. Growing up without any exposure to these awful devices made him hungry for them.

✳✳✳✳✳✳✳✳✳✳

Every time we went to the grocery store aisle with the coloring books, he'd start: "Mommy, can I have a coloring book?"

"No!" say I, the expert.

"Please..."

"No!" screams Dragon Mom.

"Just one..."

"Never! And quit bugging me!" The dragon drags him by the shirt collar, tears streaming down his face. They leave the toy aisle and enter the cereal aisle with everyone in range watching the performance. Realizing she has an audience, Dragon Mom immediately changes into Bodunky. The two are then seen strolling out of the cereal aisle eating Lucky Charms, but without a coloring book.

What was the result of all this denial? The day my son was old enough to have his first money to spend, he went straight to the toy aisle and bought himself one of the much-coveted items. He spent two days on his tummy, coloring his heart out. The next week, when he got his allowance, he bought another one!

✳✳✳✳✳✳✳✳✳✳

Oh, well. I just don't seem to learn about the effects of fanaticism. Sometimes it seems as if my expert brain is as small as my dragon one—but I love her anyway.

Back to play. Through play, children also develop the *language skills* that are essential for reading. Children learn language from adults, but they practice alone and with other children. Play provides the means for this to happen. Language development is vital to reading—reading is, after all, language. Reading involves a new set of symbols for the sounds of oral language. If you don't have the first set of oral language symbols, you can't very well learn the second.

118

I know very well that the way to help children develop oral language skills is to listen closely to them and expand on what they say. You seldom need to actually teach vocabulary. New words are introduced in actual conversations. For example, if the baby says, "Dada, bye-bye," you say, "Yes. Daddy's leaving now. See the car drive away?" If the older child says, "Danny's mother had to go to court and the guy with the hammer said she didn't have to come back," you say, "I bet she was relieved when the judge excused her from jury duty."

Knowing that careful listening was important for children to learn language, did I always do it? Of course not. Dragon Mom needs her privacy, and since she was seldom away from her small children, she learned to gain it by tuning out those childish voices. She developed such a strong habit that she still turns them off, although she's not with her children so much any more. The dragon has wonderful powers of concentration, but sadly enough, these are seldom focused on her children.

Another habit Dragon Mom developed was to go onto automatic pilot when her children talk to her. She can carry on a whole conversation without being aware of what's being said.

※※※※※※※※※

"Mommy, look what I have! I found it."

"Yeah. That's nice, honey."

"Can I keep it?'

"Sure, sweetie."

"Really?"

"Hm-mmm."

"Mom, he has my five-dollar bill! Give it back right now!"

"Mom said I could keep it. Didn't you, Mom?"

"Hmm-mm."

※※※※※※※※※

119

Dragon Mom has made some pretty big goofs on automatic pilot. She's always giving permission when she doesn't mean to. Her kids take advantage of that situation all the time.

She used to feel guilty about her lack of attention until the day she discovered that her children aren't always really talking to her. This fact became clear one day when the youngest was playing with action figures in the same room. He seemed to keep trying to draw her into the play, asking questions or making comments which she answered vaguely from the computer.

✳✳✳✳✳✳✳✳✳✳

"Mom, look what this guy can do."

"Hmmm...That's great..."

"This guy sure can climb."

"Oh, he's a good climber."

Suddenly, she realized she should be paying more attention to this child, so she started really listening, prepared to give in-depth and meaningful answers.

"Mom, watch Snag fly! Wheee!" Snag flies over the other figures, landing upside down on his head.

"Wow!" says alert Competent Mom. "He's a good flyer, isn't he? I wonder if he hurt himself when he landed." She gets close to the action, trying to make eye contact, but the boy's eyes are on the action figures.

"Look what this guy's doing!" He shoves a small figure under the edge of a pillow.

"He seems to be hiding. I wonder what he's hiding from. Is he scared? Is the other guy going to get him?" She's trying hard to get involved.

The boy moves away, walking two figures, leaving the hidden one under the pillow. He murmurs, "Hmmm" in her direction without looking up.

"What's going to happen now?" she asks in an interested voice. It's obvious that he doesn't want a conversation with her. He's on the other side of the room now, flying another guy around.

She realized then that he didn't want her to play; he was just checking in periodically. His purpose was to include her peripherally in the play, but he didn't seem to intend for her to stop typing and start a conversation. He wanted a response, but "meaningful answers" were more of an interruption than he wanted. She returned to her computer and vague answers, a little wiser about conversations with children when they're absorbed in play.

✳✳✳✳✳✳✳✳✳✳

Besides language from parents and peers, children also need a variety of experiences so that they have things to talk about. If I told you a story about a *metate* and a *molcajete*, and you had no idea what those words referred to, you wouldn't be able to get much meaning from the story. Children who lack experience have the same problem reading about creeks if they've never seen one, or buses if they have no idea what they are.

Some argue that TV can help broaden experience. Yes. And no. Television gives children false knowledge—second-hand experience that isn't concrete, and therefore not real. What children need is to explore and experience their environment. They need to learn give and take with other children. TV gives them the feeling of participating with others, but it doesn't teach the skills of real interaction with real people and objects in the environment.

Teaching and learning is a big subject, and I've talked about it in every chapter without drawing your attention to that fact. In this chapter I've specifically focused on two aspects—self-help skills, like tying shoelaces, and learning to read. I'll end this chapter with one more important area of teaching-learning—controlling aggression.

Dragon Mom is an expert on aggression, and although she certainly hasn't gained full control, she can be trusted. She's aware that she models aggressive actions as she screams, yells, and lashes out. She wishes she could just "be nice" all the time, but then she wouldn't be a dragon. If I am to love all parts of myself, I need to accept the fact that the dragon holds a lot of aggressive energy.

Is aggressive energy all bad? Of course not, but it has taken me a long time to see this. I used to think I should squelch aggression in my children, but I've come to believe it's more a matter of guiding and controlling it than squelching. I've also come to understand the difference between aggression and violence, and it's violence that I want to eliminate. I can't do that by making my children surpress their aggressive tendencies.

I get into arguments with other parents and experts when I say that I grant my children their violent instincts in fantasy. I don't believe that playing with guns leads to killing or that playing soldiers leads to war. I believe the reverse is true. Since both killing and war exist in the world, children who play at killing are playing out their fears and fantasies rather than practicing to be killers or soldiers.

They are also trying on power. Shooting someone with a plastic gun is to a four-year-old what peek-a-boo is to a one-year-old. It's a way to control someone, making them disappear, disintegrate, or fall over. Both children soon learn that their actions do not cause a permanent condition.

Adults are aware of that fact themselves, but they understand death in a different way. To them, gun play represents violence that puts a permanent end to people, and many adults are very upset when they see children play this way.

In my experience, the adults who get fanatic about their children's urges for gun play achieve the same result I did when I got

122

fanatic about coloring books. Most children can take guns or leave them, but some children who feel denied build up stronger urges than the average child. I don't see that this happens to all children, but in my experience it does happen.

I am personally opposed to guns, although I believe that there is a better chance to get them out of your system as a child if you are not denied toy guns. I certainly don't want to give the impression that I'm in favor of war. If there's to be any world at all left to pass on to our children, each of us should be working for peace in every way we can. But I don't think we work for peace by teaching children to deny their aggressive and violent feelings.

I take the approach that there is violence in the world, and in each of us. I accept that fact. I understand the fascination children have for violent fairy tales, cartoons, movies, and television programs. I screen so that the level of violence isn't beyond a child's capacity to handle it, but I don't censor as many parents do. I also monitor exposure to violence on television by limiting viewing time.

I also accept violent wishes expressed by my children. I believe that violence on the symbolic or fantasy level is okay. In an argument, I don't get upset if a child makes horrible threats. I don't say, "Oh, you don't really mean that!" I understand that the child is very angry and has chosen that way to express it. I make it clear that actual violence is not acceptable and they know that I will prevent it if necessary, but I do a lot of ignoring of minor arguments.

It seems important to point out in this chapter that what you teach isn't always what the child learns. I'm well aware that while Janet C. Parent is giving the lesson, it's Dragon Mom's ways that my children are learning because she is always lurking behind Janet's wonderful words and techniques.

If I'm going to accept my children unconditionally, love them completely, I'd better start with myself. I need to realize that Dragon Mom is the main teacher in my family, and I'm never going to be able to kill her off. (Oh, dear! What a violent thought!)

So I'd better learn to love her. That way, she has a chance to grow and become the best that she can be. I certainly can't settle for less for the main teacher of my children!

I NEVER TAUGHT MY KIDS TO FIGHT BACK

I heard this story: the pacifist mother of a four-year-old girl in day care discovered that a little boy was beating on her daughter regularly. She talked to the teachers, but they didn't seem to be able to stop the boy. One day, the girl came home with a big bruise, and the mother decided that enough was enough.

She taught her daughter to defend herself by hitting back, delivering a blow that hurt. Next time the boy hit her, she punched him and that took care of the problem. Eventually, the two became friends. Happy ending.

That story troubled me when I heard it. If I were the parent, I'd wonder why the teachers let the hitting go on for so long. Children who can't control themselves must be controlled for their own good and the safety of others. It isn't enough to respond afterwards–the teacher must be there to deflect the blow. Every time! It's up to adults to protect four-year-olds and keep them safe. I'd investigate the situation in the day care first.

Then I'd teach my child some non-violent defense techniques. One technique is to teach children to say, "Stop! I don't like it when you hit me. It hurts!" or words to that effect. That approach will work when the child hitting understands other people's feelings. Some children need to be taught that hitting hurts.

The words-only approach probably won't work if the little boy's goal is to hurt my daughter. In that case, she needs backup, which must be provided by adults. Instead of just rescuing her, teachers can support her by saying, "No!" loudly and clearly, while they stand by to protect her.

I learned other techniques from my son Adam, who made a decision as a boy not to fight back after he had landed in the principal's office a few times for defending himself. He says, "You can sometimes act as if the threat is so ridiculous it isn't worth attention. Your message is, "Me fight you? You must be kidding!"

Adam also developed a keen nose for danger. He learned to avoid situations where he was vulnerable. He took friends with him to places where being a loner might make him a target.

I do not advocate teaching children to hit, even in self-defense. I do advocate teaching non-violent alternatives. I also urge all adults in charge of young children to protect them. It's sad when a four-year-old comes to see the world as a dangerous place!

125

CONCLUSION

This chapter is about love. In fact, the whole book is about love. It's easy to see Bodunky as loving, or you may think that Janet Competent Parent is the loving one because she has better ideas about how to parent. But in truth it's Dragon Mom who has the giant share of love. The feeling fibers that make up the creature's huge muscular structure are full of love. In fact, the dragon is almost pure feeling. The intensity of her storms is directly related to her capacity to love. She's a passionate creature.

Janet Competent Parent loves and Bodunky does too, of course. The only one of my characters that doesn't hold much love is the expert. She thinks rather than feels. That approach used to seem good to me. Feeling is so unpredictable—so liable to get out of hand. When you're feeling, you're more likely to behave in ways you don't approve of!

I thought being a cool, dispassionate, *reasonable* parent was my ultimate goal. I know differently now. My expert is well-informed and intelligent, but she's a lousy parent. She lacks spontaneity and she's far too intellectual. She's got plenty of brains, but no guts. Good parenting comes from the gut, not the head.

Of course the good parent learns with her head, taking in information that improves her skills. But she can't act primarily from the intellect. Even when you try hard to change, parenting actions come straight from the midsection with just a little direction from the head.

Love is definitely a gut reaction. No one's brain ever created real love. Knowing that love is not a created condition, the question arises: how does parent love start? Some experts will tell you that parent-child love comes from bonding—that magical moment right after birth when parent and child first meet. I say, "Baloney!" Some couples fall in love at

126

first sight, sure. Some parents and babies do too. But whether or not you have a wham-bang beginning, it takes time to build a real relationship.

I don't mean to deny the bonding concept. I've seen a lot of good come from it. Getting off to a good start is always better than getting off to a bad start, which is what old-fashioned hospital procedures used to promote.

✳✳✳✳✳✳✳✳✳✳

"Well, here's your baby, Mrs. Jones. It's a boy." Baby is dangling upside down, screaming, just out of reach.

"No, don't touch. You'll get to hold him when we get him cleaned and wrapped up, but then only for a minute because he has to go to the nursery. Your husband? Oh, yes, we'll tell him. I assume he's still in the waiting room. I'm sure he'll be happy it's all over."

✳✳✳✳✳✳✳✳✳✳

Times have changed. Babies are now regarded as human from the start, and effort is usually made to let the newborn and parents get acquainted right away. Many parents and babies do fall in love at first sight, and this bonding period is a real bonus to them.

With all the emphasis on bonding these days, I worry about what happens to parents who, for various reasons, cannot share those first moments. Do they give up on loving their child? I hope not.

Most adults alive today who were born in the United States did not have that special bonding period with their parents at birth, yet plenty of them grew up feeling closely attached to their parents, and their parents to them. A shared beginning in a calm, loving atmosphere is wonderful, but not absolutely essential for attachment.

Bonding was not a familiar concept when my three oldest sons arrived. The medical world was still busy applying technology to the birthing process. Psychological matters were less worried about. Three of my first four babies arrived in sterile delivery rooms. They were immediately bundled off to be cared for by experts during their first "fragile" hours. My ability to care for them was hampered by my lack of expertise in a hospital setting and by my somewhat drugged condition.

The other of my first four babies was born across the world in entirely different– but unknown–circumstances. She was found on a street corner in Hong Kong when she was about five days old, then placed in a poverty-stricken orphanage where the major concern was finding enough for the children to eat. No one, I am sure, worried in the least about bonding.

She arrived in this country to be my daughter just before the end of her second year. I remember my feelings of anticipation at the airport waiting for her flight to arrive, the culmination of a more-than-two-year adoption process full of frustrations and setbacks.

✳✳✳✳✳✳✳✳✳✳

I was in a state of heightened excitement when the first passengers stepped through the doors into the waiting room. I noticed that I was holding my breath. Would I recognize my new daughter? I had only one picture, and it was thirteen months out of date. A man appeared, holding a toddler in each arm. I let my breath out. The child in his left arm was mine! I rushed to him, waving a piece of paper that gave me claim to this child.

"That's my child," I managed to gasp, reaching out for her.

Ignoring my outstretched arms, he set her carefully on the floor. She balanced unsteadily on her patent leather shoes. Her eyes were fixed on his knees. The man bent over to look at a plastic band around her wrist, matching the name to the one on the paper I held up to his face. He seemed uncertain. I wasn't.

"She's my daughter," I explained patiently. He looked from the paper to the plastic bracelet once again. Still he hesitated. He squinted, rereading carefully.

128

"Yes," he said shortly, finally agreeing that she was indeed who I thought she was. Picking her up once again, he handed her into my waiting arms.

I hugged her and whispered, "Hello," in her tiny ear. She looked at me through half-closed eyes. There was no emotion on her face.

In those days before car seats, I was able to hold my new daughter in the car on the way home. She seemed dazed. She uttered not a single sound, nor showed any expression on her face. She fell asleep, but woke again when the car stopped. It was late at night, and she seemed sleepy, so I put her to bed soon after we arrived home. At first, she stood up in her new crib, looking without interest at her surroundings. When I laid her down, she stayed there and went right to sleep.

✳✳✳✳✳✳✳✳✳

That was the beginning of our relationship. There was no magical moment of bonding between us. I certainly had some feelings, but hers were deeply buried. They didn't begin to emerge for weeks.

Robin, as I called her, began to recognize her new family after a few days, but she didn't seem particularly partial to any of us for some time after that. I remember once walking down the street and feeling her let go of my hand. She walked straight to a woman sitting on a bench waiting for a bus. Without hesitation, she climbed up on the woman's lap and sat there looking around. A year later, she was still sitting on the laps of strangers without being invited. It was as if laps called out to her and it didn't matter whose they were.

It wasn't long, however, before she became attached to me in a normal way. She would protest when I left her to go out in the evening, just as my other two children had done at her age. Eventually you couldn't tell us from any other mother and daughter, except that we don't look alike, because we're of different races.

129

In 1979, when Child Number Five came along, I had great expectations for the birth. The hospital and I knew about unmedicated delivery and the importance of shared beginnings. I planned to make the most of our first meeting. But fate had other plans.

✳✳✳✳✳✳✳✳✳✳

My last son was born three months early. I remember every moment of his short birth. Afterwards, I stared at the ceiling of the labor room. Although he was still on the bed between my knees, I didn't want to see him. I was convinced he was dead. If I hadn't been so numb, I'd have cried my eyes out. So much for my expectations of bonding.

The next time I saw my two-pound baby, he was attached to a machine that was doing his breathing for him. He lay with a tube disappearing into his mouth behind white tape. His eyes were open. I thought he looked at me. I wasn't sure.

"You can touch him," the doctor said kindly. The tiny naked body lay there quite available under the heat lamps. No sterile blanket kept my skin from his like with my other newborn sons. I slowly reached out and gingerly touched his miniature foot. I winced. I drew my hand back. The doctor looked at me. I reached out again. This time, I held onto his foot, which was cool to my touch.

During the long hospital stay, I was well aware of protecting myself from getting too attached to this baby. His prognosis was bad. They didn't think he would make it, and if he did survive, the chances were not good that he would ever live a normal life. I didn't *consciously* distance myself from my child, but I did distance myself.

All of that changed when he came home from the hospital. But, as with my other children, the relationship grew over time. It didn't happen in a single, magical moment at birth.

✳✳✳✳✳✳✳✳✳✳

Although I love each of my children, I have a different relationship with each one. I never measure love. Love is unique just as each child is unique. I don't compare children, and I don't compare my love.

That certainly sounds very mature and admirable. But you'll wonder about me if you ever drop by when the dragon is stamping around, ranting, raving, and crushing everything in her path. You'll question whether I have the capacity to love at all. Let me assure you, I do. Dragon Mom wouldn't get so angry if love weren't behind the passion. Parenting is an emotional experience; there's no doubt about that. And Dragon Mom is an emotional creature.

It's no coincidence that I chose a dragon image for the monster inside me. I like dragons' ferocity, that instinctual power which strikes fear into the hearts of those who worry about wildness.

I used to be scared to death of the monster in me. Even though I continually proved to myself that her razor claws and fire breath wouldn't harm my children, I didn't want to be a dragon. I wanted to be calm and rational all the time. I couldn't stand the unpredictable power that came over me during intense moments.

I don't fear wildness anymore. My uncivilized dragon reminds me that I am as much a part of nature as it is a part of me. My dragon self kept me going during a long period before I began to wake up to who I am and what I need.

I remember a period of deadness about myself. I performed the functions expected of a wife, mother, daughter, and preschool teacher to the best of my ability, but there was something missing. I did things mechanically, numbly. I was alive, but not vital. I focused my attention, but not clearly. I had energy, but I wasn't lively.

A constant nervousness prodded me to keep busy. If I ever slowed down, I felt uncomfortable, even panicky. I performed, I produced, I made people happy, but I wasn't happy. I wasn't sad, either.

In fact, I didn't feel much of anything, *except* when I raged as Dragon Mom. When the rage came, the numbness disappeared, my sight cleared up, and a powerful energy filled my body.

Now Dragon Mom's power and energy is always available to me when I need it. I don't have to rant and rave. Dragon energy wakes me up and makes me feel. I'm still not all the way awake, but I'm seldom numb any more. I do have periods when I'm fully conscious instead of only half there.

I'm beginning to appreciate full-bodied awareness in quiet moments as well as intense ones. I'm learning to live mindfully, to *pay attention* and *take care* in the fullest sense of those words. I can detect when I'm doing one thing and thinking about a million other things. I don't always stop to appreciate the moment, but I'm aware that I can.

We each have a dragon in us. It may take different forms or behave in individual ways, but the dragon holds a kind of power that is vital to our health. We may have to journey to the depths of our darkest parts to get in touch with this life force, but it's there.

I know now that I've been on a dragon quest all my life. I'm getting closer to her lair than I've ever been before. At times I'm able to risk enough to get in touch with this beast inside me. When we finally come face to face, I won't try to kill her. The hunt has a different purpose now. When I meet her, I will feed her chocolate cake. It will be my way of saying, "I love you!"–to myself.